WILTON
WEDDINGS

Every bride wants a wedding day that lives up to her dreams—with the perfect setting, a beautiful ceremony, a wonderful menu and more. There is so much to be done, so many decisions to be made, it is difficult to know where to begin.

Wilton Weddings is a great place to start your personal wedding plan. Not every couple can afford a professional wedding consultant. This book is filled with the expert advice you need to create a celebration that is ideal for you.

Use *Wilton Weddings* from day one. The size and style of reception, how much to spend, how to best arrange your reception space, what to serve—these are just some of the questions you will find answers for here. This book will organize you, with a special pull-out planner that includes a month-by-month agenda and a convenient budget table you can refer to right up to the big day.

Wilton Weddings is also designed to inspire you. You'll see great ways to dress up the reception—whether your setting is a backyard garden, an elegant hotel or the home of a relative. And, of course, you'll choose from many exciting Wilton cake designs to suit the style and size of your wedding.

Planning your wedding will be one of the most exciting times of your life. We hope that this book will help make the days leading up to your wedding day easier and more enjoyable. I wish you all the best as you celebrate a wonderful wedding and begin a new future.

Vince Naccarato

Vince Naccarato
President

CONTENTS

WEDDING CAKES

*Let our dramatic collection of cake designs inspire you. Whatever your reception
style or size, you will find a design to complement it...Victorian, Contemporary or Traditional.
Complete decorating instructions and diagrams included.*

PLANNING THE RECEPTION

*Use these sections as a "wedding workbook", designed to put you in control of every detail.
We provide advice and offer you options for three popular reception settings, helping you organize the
location, create the budget, write the guest list, select the menu and much more.*

WEDDING PRODUCTS

*The essential trims and tools for making your cake look beautiful.
Exquisite ornaments and accents, quality pan sets, cake stands, pillars, keepsakes and more.*

SWEET
REVERIE

*A work of textural art, as intricate cornelli lace is complemented
by our scrolled garden stand. Serves 114.*

ACCESSORIES YOU'LL NEED:

- 4-Pc. Oval Pan Set (10¾ x 7⅞ in., 13 x 9⅞ in., 16 x 12⅜ in. used)
- Tips 2, 16, 18, 22, 104
- Cake Boards, Fanci-Foil Wrap
- Garden Cake Stand
- 10, 14, 18 in. Separator Plates (1 each)
- Scallop Patterns (p. 128-131)
- Fresh Flower Holders (2 pkgs. needed)
- Fresh flowers, greenery
- Ornament: *New Beginning*

Cut oval shaped boards and cover with foil. Ice 2-layer cakes smooth. Using toothpick, mark Scallop Pattern on cake sides.

Imprint oval pattern on cake tops: Use 7¾ x 5⅝ in. oval pan as pattern for top of 13 x 9⅞ in. cake and 10¾ x 7⅞ in. oval pan as pattern for top of 16 x 12⅜ in. cake.

Pipe tip 2 cornelli lace on all cakes. Pipe tip 18 shell border on cake top around imprinted ovals. Pipe tip 104 swags; around scallops add tip 16 zigzags. Add tip 16 rosettes at point of each garland. Pipe tip 22 shell bottom borders on all cakes.

At reception, position cakes on stand. Add ornament, flowers in flower holder and greenery.

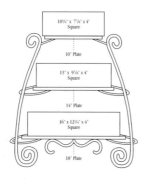

DOVES WILL SOAR

Lovely roses and elegant doves place this smaller-scale cake in a class of its own. It's a design that allows for relaxed decorating...once covered, the rolled fondant cakes can be stored at room temperature up to four days, and the royal icing roses can be made months in advance. Serves 77.

ACCESSORIES YOU'LL NEED:

- 8, 14 in. Round Pans
- Tips 2, 3, 4, 5, 6, 7, 10, 12, 16, 101, 101s, 102, 103, 104, 172, 352
- Flower Nail No. 7
- Ivory, Juniper Green Icing Colors
- Ready-To-Use Rolled Fondant (3 packages needed)
- Garland Pattern, p. 133
- Cake Dividing Set
- Dowel Rods
- Meringue Powder
- Cake Board, Fanci-Foil Wrap
- Small Doves (1 pkg. needed)
- Royal & Buttercream Icings, p. 118
- Ornament: *Circles of Love*

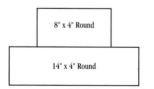

Using royal icing, make 64 roses: 8 tip 104 with tip 12 bases; 16 tip 103 with tip 10 bases; 16 tip 102 with tip 7 bases; 16 tip 101 with tip 5 bases; 8 tip 101s with tip 3 bases. Let dry.

Make garlands in advance: Cover Garland Pattern with waxed paper. With royal icing, pipe tip 16 zigzag to form garland. Eight garlands will be needed (make extras to allow for breakage). Let dry.

When garlands and roses are dry, attach roses to garlands with royal icing. Postion tip 104 rose in center, tip 103 second, tip 102 third, tip 101 fourth. Pipe tip 352 leaves. (Tip 101s roses will be placed directly on cake to join each garland later.)

Prepare 2-layer cakes for rolled fondant (p. 119) and stacked construction (p. 113).

With cake dividing set, divide 8 in. cake into 8ths and mark 3 inches up from bottom of cake. Divide 14 in. cake into 8ths; mark a center area between each division for drop strings, 3 in. wide and 3 in. up from bottom of cake. For both cakes pipe triple drop strings, 1¾ in. from bottom at lowest point: use tip 6 for bottom string, tip 4 for middle string and tip 2 for top string. Pipe tip 2 dots at points. Pipe tip 172 bottom shell borders trimmed with tip 4 zigzags on both cakes. Add tip 2 double drop strings on bottom zigzag border of 8 in. cake.

At reception, position rose garlands at division marks. Add tip 101s roses above meeting point of garlands. Using icing, attach doves above tip 101s roses. Add tip 352 leaves on roses. Position ornament.

FILIGREE FANTASY

This chocolate lover's dream has a distinctive look and a decadent flavor. Rich chocolate buttercream, coupled with lacy candy arches, creates a match made in heaven. Serves 108.

ACCESSORIES YOU'LL NEED:

- 6, 7, 8, 10, 12, 14 in. Round Pans
- Tips 1, 2, 16, 17, 18
- 4 Pc. Floating Tiers Cake Stand Set
- Lt. Cocoa Candy Melts®* (6 bags needed)
- 7 x 6½ in. Filigree Heart Frame
- Romantic Heart Base, 3¼ in. diameter
- Cake Dividing Set
- Decorator Brush Set
- Disposable Decorating Bags
- Chocolate Buttercream Icing, p. 118
- Small, Medium, Large Filigree Patterns, p. 135

* brand confectionery coating

Make candy filigree pieces at least one day ahead of time. You will need 84 small, 12 medium and 12 large pieces (make extra to allow for breakage). Place waxed paper over patterns. Pipe tip 1 small filigree and tip 2 medium and large filigree patterns on waxed paper; chill in refrigerator 5-10 minutes. Remove from paper, turn over and overpipe on reverse side. Refrigerate to set. Set aside in cool area.

Paint filigree heart and heart base using melted Candy Melts and decorator brush. Outline hearts on base with melted candy using disposable bag fitted with tip 1. Refrigerate to set.

Ice 1-layer cakes smooth and prepare for stacked construction. Using the cake dividing set, divide 6, 8, 12 in. rounds into 12ths and 7, 10, 14 in. rounds into 24ths. For 6 and 7 in. cakes, pipe tip 16 stars on top and bottom borders; for 8 and 10 in. cakes, pipe tip 17 star borders; for 12 and 14 in. cakes, pipe tip 18 star borders.

At reception, position filigree pieces at division marks: small pieces on side of 6 in., 7 in., 10 in. and 14 in. tiers; medium filigree pieces on top of 8 in. tier and large filigree pieces on top of 12 in. tier. Position filigree heart on top of cake.

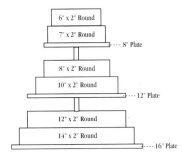

BOUNTIFUL BLESSINGS

Each basketweave tier overflows with fresh seasonal fruits, creating a cake alive with color and beauty. Don't let your beautiful berries and grapes go to waste—when cutting the cake, add fruit to each serving plate. Serves 272.

ACCESSORIES YOU'LL NEED:

- 8, 10, 12, 14 in. Round Pans
- Tips 2B, 18, 21
- Tall Tier Stand Plates: five 10 in.; one each: 12 in., 14 in., 16 in.
- Tall Tier Stand Columns: four 6½ in.
- Tall Tier 4-Arm Base Stand
- Top Column Cap Nut
- Cake Corer Tube
- Cake Boards, Fanci-Foil Wrap
- Meringue Powder
- Frolicking Cherubs (4 needed)
- Silk Ivy Leaves
- Fresh grapes, strawberries, sugar
- Ornament: *Hearts Take Wing*

Prepare and ice 2-layer cakes with buttercream icing. Pipe tip 2B basketweave on all cakes. Add tip 18 top shell borders to each tier, then add tip 21 bottom shell borders to all tiers except one 8 in. cake.

Morning of reception: dip fruit in meringue wash and coat with granulated sugar (see recipe below).

At reception, bolt 6½ in. column to 4-arm base with bottom column bolt, add 16 in. plate with 6½ in. column, then add 14 in. plate with 6½ in. column, then 12 in. plate with 6½ in. column. Anchor 10 in. plate with column cap nut, position 8 in. tier and add tip 21 bottom shell border. Position cherubs, sugared fruit, silk leaves and ornament.

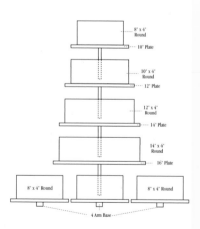

SUGARED FRUIT

- 4 Teaspoons Meringue Powder or Color Flow Mix
- ¼ Cup Water
- ⅓ Cup Sugar

In a small bowl beat meringue powder or color flow mix and water with fork. Wash and blot fruit dry; brush meringue mixture on fruit with a pastry brush. Place sugar in a small fine mesh strainer and sprinkle on fruit. Let dry on cooling grid. Grapes can remain at room temperature 4-5 hours, strawberries and raspberries 2-3 hours.

A LOVE FOR THE AGES

The fine art of color flow—"drawing" in icing—enables you to capture the dimensions of each rose petal with breathtaking clarity. The technique is easy, using the patterns in this book and Color Flow Mix. The plaques can be prepared well in advance of the reception. Serves 72.

ACCESSORIES YOU'LL NEED:

- 15 in. Hexagon Pan
- 8 in. Round Pan
- Tips 2, 3, 363
- Aster Mauve, Juniper Green Icing Colors
- Love Plaque, Single Rose, Rose Cluster Patterns, p. 132
- Color Flow Mix
- Cake Dividing Set
- Cake Boards, Fanci-Foil Wrap
- 9 in. Crystal-Look Plates (2 needed)
- 7 in. Crystal-Look Pillars (1 pkg. needed)
- Crystal-Look Bowl (1 needed)
- Ready-To-Use Rolled Fondant (5 pkgs. needed)
- Buttercream, Color Flow Icings, p. 118-119
- Fresh Flowers
- Ornament: *Sweetness*

Using Color Flow Icing, Tip 2 and Patterns, make 1 Love Plaque, 8 Single Roses and 5 Rose Clusters. Outline using full strength Color Flow Icing (reserve ¼ cup full-strength color flow to attach pieces to fondant cake). Let dry, then flow in centers. Make extras to allow for breakage and let dry.

Prepare 2-layer round and 2-layer hexagon tiers for rolled fondant and pillar construction.

15 in. tier: Pipe tip 363 bottom shell border and around Crystal-Look Plate.

8 in. tier: Using Cake Dividing Set, dot mark cake into 8ths, ¾ in. down from edge. Using tip 3, pipe triple drop strings 2 in. wide and 2½ in. deep, beginning and ending ½ in. on each side of division marks. Pipe tip 363 bottom shell border.

At reception, position color flow pieces using dots of color flow on the back and attach to cake. Assemble cakes on pillars. Position ornament and fresh flowers in bowl.

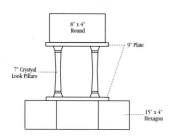

8" x 4"
Round

9" Plate

7" Crystal
Look Pillars

15" x 4"
Hexagon

THE
GARDEN
WEDDING

No other setting captures the natural beauty, romance

and magic of a wedding celebration quite like that of

the garden. Her vibrant colors and lush green foliage make

Mother Nature the perfect hostess for such a grand event.

Whether your ideal setting is a large formal garden or

a more intimate home garden, there are a few important

things to remember. Along with the splendor of the

outdoors comes a host of interesting challenges and

unique risks. Most often the risks you take are well worth

it, but remember, your wedding dreams are more likely

to come true if you are thorough in your planning,

creative in your approach and most of all, flexible.

The **beauty** of the
garden can make your wedding day
an unforgettable celebration.

PLANNING AND "PLANTING" AHEAD

You've heard it a thousand times, "organization is the key to a successful wedding." But when planning a garden wedding, this is not just good advice—it's a necessity. After all, preparing for a garden wedding is a bit more complicated than simply booking a banquet hall—it may even mean getting your hands in the dirt!

Choosing your wedding colors early is important when planning a garden wedding, so let your garden help you. Consider the colors of the plants that will be in bloom at the time of your wedding and build your color scheme around them. Don't choose colors that will compete with your garden flowers, and don't attempt to re-design the colors of an existing garden. Simply identify the most prominent colors of the flowers that will be in bloom and then choose your accent colors to complement them. Be sure to consider the season and surrounding trees, also. Yellows, reds, golds, and bronzes will drape the background of an early Fall wedding, while pinks and whites from flowering trees may highlight the late Spring wedding.

During planting season, keep your upcoming wedding in mind. The more you plant ahead of time, the less you will have to bring in on your wedding day. A good idea is to plant extra flower beds that will bloom in white or in the colors that reflect your overall theme. Extra planting effort will not only give you additional control over your colors, but will ensure your garden is rich and dense. You should also have some idea of the reception layout when planting your garden. The areas where your guests will spend most of their time should be the prettiest and may require more careful attention.

WHAT GOES WHERE? PLANNING YOUR SPACE

Once you've selected your garden space, you should begin mapping out your event. This is a great opportunity to get creative and is also a good time to design the ever-important "Plan B" in case of inclement weather.

You will first want to consider the number of guests you plan on inviting and whether the dinner will be plated or buffet style. In any event, your guest area should be covered—and so should your food. You or your caterer should invite a tent expert out to the site to measure your space and make suggestions regarding tent sizes and styles. You will also want to inquire about flooring. If the grass area for your guests is level for the most part, you may be able to get away with flooring only the dance floor and music areas—if there is no rain and the ground is solid. To be on the safe side, you may want to floor the entire tent. Although it can be costly, it can also prevent unfortunate mishaps such as sprained ankles or sinking pump heels. Most often, it's money well spent.

After you have planned out your guest area, your next space of concern should be your food preparation area. This is something you should discuss in great detail with your caterer or with whomever is preparing your meal, since everyone has his or her own special needs. For many garden weddings, a clean cleared-out garage makes a great food prep area. It provides shelter and is separated from your guests. If no garage is available, then you will need at least a 30' x 30' cook tent for food preparation. As with the garage, you will want to erect the tent in an area that will not be accessible to your guests. One of the biggest drawbacks of a garden wedding is that often there is no access to refrigerators or ovens, unlike a hotel or banquet wedding. That means you will have to allow extra space for grills and refrigeration units to be brought in with the caterer. To save time and space on the day of your wedding, your caterer should arrive with much of the food already prepared, (vegetables pre-cut, meat seasoned, etc.) But the food prep staff will need plenty of space to assemble plated meals or the buffet menu. Be sure to provide a number of preparation tables so your staff can be as efficient as possible and consult with the caterer or family friends who have offered help to determine their needs.

In addition to your cooking and food prep areas, you will need to designate space for the following: buffet table, hors d'oeuvres table, cake table, music, gift table, bar area, and dessert table. If space is tight, your catering staff can serve hors d'oeuvres and bring gifts to the main house, instead of having separate tables. Be sure to consider traffic patterns when assigning these stations, also. You don't want to underestimate the space needed for the areas where people are most likely to mingle, such as the bar or hors d'oeuvres stations. Notice that for our "gift table" we have used an old-fashioned iron loveseat. Wooden garden benches, or porch swings make charming spots for guests to leave their beautifully wrapped gifts.

OTHER PLANNING CONSIDERATIONS

• Plan B: Shelter in case of severe weather
• Parking (self-park or valet)
• Electrical needs of caterer, D.J., etc.
• Transition lighting into evening— torches, candles, etc.
• Insects
• Restroom Accessibility
• Staffing Requirements
• Special needs for children, elderly, or handicapped

First of all, try to think of as many things that can go wrong and write them on a list. Then for each possibility, figure out what you or your event helpers will do to either prevent them from happening at all, or at the very least, prepare a recovery plan if something should go wrong.

For a garden wedding, weather should be your biggest concern. A well-tented and floored garden reception should reduce the possibilities of disaster. However, severe storms, and unexpected and excessive heat or cold are possibilities—and even the best tent may not provide enough protection.

If you want a 100 percent guarantee against Mother Nature, be sure your garden is accompanied by indoor shelter that can accommodate your guests. In other words, you should be prepared to move the entire celebration indoors. (See At-Home Reception sectionon p. 40 for more ideas on weddings at home.)

Talk to recent brides who had similar garden receptions—ask what worked? What didn't?

As with any wedding, your attention to detail is what makes your day your very own. There's no doubt that your creative ideas coupled with good planning and a little luck from Mother Nature will bring you a wedding day to remember always. Here's wishing you warm sunshine, gentle breezes and all the beauty of the garden.

For an outside summer wedding, where flowers are exposed to heat and direct sunlight, be sure to choose hardy garden cuts, such as larkspur, delphinium, and lilies. Tropical flowers, such as orchids, anthirium, and birds of paradise also hold up well in the heat. Potted flowers hold up the best. Stay away from bulb cuts such as tulips, iris and jonquils if you expect your flowers to last in day-long sun.

FLOWERS, FLOWERS AND MORE FLOWERS!

Although your garden setting will naturally take care of your flower needs, you will no doubt want to add some ideas of your own. You will most likely require the services of a professional florist to handle all of your finishing touches. When choosing your florist, be sure to look for someone who truly understands your overall style and theme. Choose someone who is creative AND knowledgeable—and be sure to review his/her portfolio book. Ask to see the photos of any other garden weddings they have been hired to do.

Together with your florist you will first decide how many separate arrangements you will need, including guest table centerpieces, buffet arrangement, wedding party bouquets, boutonnieres, head table, bride's bouquet, dessert table, cake table, hanging and potted plants. Choose three or four dominant flowers that will appear in each arrangement. Then choose accent flowers to be added to each— these should complement your garden flowers.

As you begin your flower selection, you will soon discover that there are endless possibilities. To accent our garden's natural pink and purple hues, we have chosen rubrum lilies, white iris, statice, and Queen Ann's Lace to be our primary flowers. An important objective is to choose flowers that will hold up well and fill space. Flowers with large vibrant blooms offer you the most for your money. Smaller blooming flowers such as violets and lily of the valley may look nice close-up, but aren't practical when you require multiple arrangements to fill space and produce lots of color.

As beautiful as the garden is, sometimes Mother Nature's timing isn't always in sync with our party-plan-

ning, so we have "enhanced" the garden by adding cut flowers to the flower beds. Since the color scheme in this garden emphasizes tones of pink and purple with highlights of blue and yellow, our florist has brought in colorful bunches of tall delphinium, Queen Ann's Lace, and larkspur. These lovely cuts have been carefully nestled among the existing flowers to add additional color in areas that are sparse or where the garden has not yet bloomed. Be careful not to overdo it with extra plants or your garden will look too staged. Your goal is to bring in just enough for added color while still maintaining the garden's natural balance.

Remember, with a garden wedding, there is no need for overkill when it comes to flowers. Your setting will be naturally elegant because of the garden alone; that's why you chose a garden wedding to begin with! So don't let yourself get carried away, let the garden do the work for you . . . simplicity will yield stunning results.

FLOWER IDEAS WORTH PONDERING . . . LET YOUR CREATIVITY SOAR!

Here are just a few ideas to get you started . . .

• White, pink, or red geraniums are as lovely as they are hardy. Try potting them and accenting with colorful fabric ribbon for centerpieces. They also make wonderful keepsakes for guests or special friends. Mini pots with small flowers make charming favors.

• A dense gathering of wild flowers in white or natural wicker baskets creates a light, natural look for the casual garden wedding.

• Clay pots of all sizes and shapes can be sprayed white to hold large flowering plants. This is a great alternative to large arrangements, and will also live well beyond your wedding day.

• Flowering hanging baskets bring color to a higher level and fill awkward gaps. Accent with ribbon or candles for added flair—but be sure baskets don't obstruct traffic flow.

• Remember, mixing yard flowers with more costly flowers from your florist is a great way to stretch your floral budget. Not to mention that flowers given to you from family and friends can add a very special wedding day sentiment. Yard flowers that lend themselves to arrangements, include: Queen Ann's Lace, Day Lilies, Yarrow, Delphinium, Asters, Snap Dragons, Iris, Zinnias, and Moss Roses.

• Flowers aren't your only means to add color to your buffet table. Try filling clean wooden crates, ceramic bowls, or bushel baskets with fresh produce from a farmer's market such as, tomatoes, yellow and red peppers, apples, peaches, or red and green grapes. You can even prop them on their sides slightly for a cascading effect that will add freshness and color to any garden meal!

• Garlanding is a great technique for masking trouble spots. Ivy or asparagus ferns wrapped around tent poles and ropes makes an attractive and functional cover-up. You can also use ribbon to hide poles or electrical cords. White accordion screens in the garden area or food prep area will keep guests away from dangerous or unsightly areas.

RIBBONS

A fun and cost-effective way to add color to your garden wedding is to creatively accent with ribbons. There are about as many colors of ribbon to choose from as there are flowers! For a festive-looking deck area, we have chosen a wide ribbon trio of pink, lavender and purple which accent our garden flowers and raspberry-colored linens. Each ribbon color is swaged between posts and then attached with white floral wire. After this is completed around the entire perimeter of the deck, a ribbon cluster is added to each post. To create each cluster, a ribbon streamer of each color is looped once, pinched in the center and held closed with floral wire. This separate cluster is then attached to each post. You may substitute bows or small, pre-made flower bouquets in place of the ribbon cluster for a fancier look. What a great way to add exploding color at very little cost!

LINENS

Linens play a huge part in adding color and setting the tone of your wedding. However, that doesn't mean they should steal the show! Your linens should simply complement your flowers and accent the dominant colors in your garden. Like everything else, you will have numerous colors, patterns and textures from which to choose. A good rule of thumb is, when in doubt...choose solids. You don't want your linens to compete with your garden. Floral patterns may prove to be redundant, busy, and too seasonal, they are also harder to match with other table elements such as centerpieces and china.

For a casual wedding, a single lace or solid cloth on each table is simple and appropriate. However, a very popular and attractive option for a more formal garden wedding is a solid white

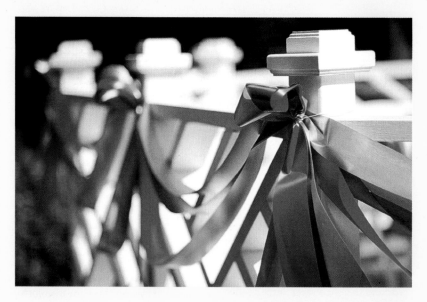

Our trio of ribbon colors accents garden flowers and complements table linens.

bottom cloth with a colorful overlay. A white bottom cloth makes a clean, crisp presentation appropriate for a wedding. Choosing your overlay is where you can get creative and have some fun! Select bright solids, as we have, or stop in at your local fabric store and look at chiffon, eyelet, or other lace fabrics to serve as your overlay. Since your overlay doesn't have to touch the ground, simply cut 56" to 60" squares of the fabric for each table (pinking the edges will prevent the fabric from unraveling). Many times this option will save you money as opposed to renting the overlays—especially if you can find fabric at $3.00-$4.00 per yard. You may even want to ask your linen service or florist if they would want to buy the linens at reduced price when the wedding is over.

Don't forget your napkins. They can match or contrast your cloth, or you can even introduce a subtle floral pattern for a fancier look. Be sure to order enough for your guests and for

bread baskets, etc. Your local library or caterer may have resources which illustrate different folding techniques.

DRAPING TECHNIQUES

Draping a table is more difficult and time-consuming than it may seem. So be sure to have enough help on hand if you are not having a caterer handle the dressing of the tables. As seen here, each of our guest tables is draped with a round white cloth. (be sure your grass is dry before laying bottom cloth) Next our bright raspberry solid overlay is added. At even intervals around the table, the top cloth has been gathered and pinned to create a dramatic and elegant look. To do this simply begin a tight gather at the floor edge of the table and secure with a pin.

The number of gatherings is what will determine how loose the overall draping will appear around each table. For a fresh, romantic touch we have attached a small table cluster of flowers consisting of brush ivy, sea foam statice, and fever few, to the top of each swag. You can add a simple rosette or ribbon cluster for a more cost effective option. White garden chairs are then placed evenly around each table.

RIBBONS

Add color to your garden wedding in a fun and inexpensive way! Beautiful ribbons make it a more festive event.

1

INCH RIBBONS IN CENTER

TIE RIBBONS TOGETHER WITH FLORAL WIRE

3

ATTACH BOW AT EACH POST WITH FLORAL WIRE

4

DRAPING

BEGIN A TIGHT GATHER AT FLOOR EDGE OF TABLE

1

SECURE GATHERED FABRIC WITH A PIN

Draping techniques can give your guest tables an elegant and dramatic look. Attaching flowers to top of swags adds to the romance of the day.

FLOWERS CAN BE ADDED TO THE TOP OF EACH SWAG

3

LOOP RIBBON STREAMER

BRIDE & GROOM'S TABLE

At many weddings, the bride and groom share the head table with their bridal party. But for a more intimate garden setting, we have set our bride and groom off in a lovely shaded section of the garden. This small table-for-two has been specially dressed for the happy couple to set them apart from the rest of the wedding. To designate this as the bride and groom's table, our florist has created a romantic spray featuring stunning large Casablanca lilies, white iris and ivy to drape across the front of the table. Each chair is then accented with a small bouquet of lilies, white iris, and sheer white ribbon. This is sure to be a wedding meal to remember.

CHINA & GLASSWARE

When choosing your china—keep it simple. Your garden, flowers, ribbons, and linen will do a more than adequate job of introducing color and creating a festive setting. A solid white plate is most appropriate for a wedding and will show off your food the best. We have chosen a large white buffet plate with embossed detailing around the rim. The larger sized plate is important if you are planning a buffet. This gives your guests plenty of room to space out their food when serving themselves.

*Note: Plates are photographed on tables to show complete table setting, however, buffet plates are typically stacked at the buffet table.

In addition to dinner plates, you will need to order cups, saucers and dessert plates. Glassware, such as water goblets, wine, champagne and punch bowl/glasses, should also be ordered at this time along with silverware.

YOUR MENU

Since weddings have traditionally been a time to eat, drink, and be merry, everything on your menu deserves careful consideration—right down to the last breadstick. Your garden theme should encourage you to select a menu that features fresh, seasonal, colorful foods, and at the same time is sensible for serving outdoors.

Perhaps the two most important things to remember when choosing your menu—aside from quality first— is to serve foods that will hold up well in outdoor conditions and that will require minimal preparation time the day of your event. Your menu selection will depend on the time of day your guests will be eating. A late morning or early afternoon brunch may feature fresh omelets, bakery goods, smoked meats, fresh fruits and juices. A luncheon menu may offer a variety of salads, canapes, and a simple filet of chicken, fish, or lean beef. We have chosen a country supper menu which

has been designed to complement our garden setting while offering entrees and side dishes that can easily be made ahead of time, with minimal preparation or risk of spoilage. Heat is a major consideration when planning your garden menu. Don't use recipes which contain ingredients that will spoil under extreme conditions such as mayonnaise or seafood. Items that will hold up well in hot weather include: pasta salad with vinaigrette dressing, hardy vegetable salads, marinated salads, rice dishes, or smoked meats and fish.

If your caterer will be handling your menu, you can leave it up to him or her to worry about food preparation—that's the expertise you're paying for! However, we have intentionally designed our menu to be prepared without needing a formal caterer. With a little patience and a lot of organization you can prepare a scrumptious meal simply by enlisting the help of family and friends. If you are planning a buffet meal, do not expect one 6 to 8 foot buffet to serve more than 50 guests, or they will be waiting in line. Two identical buffets are recommended to keep the line moving. Remember, too, that your buffet should feature your main meal only—and not include dessert. Your dessert table should be separate to avoid overcrowded plates and mixing foods that don't belong together.

WHEN PREPARING FOOD ON YOUR OWN:

- Choose recipes that can be duplicated appropriately for the number of guests you are serving. Not all recipes are designed to serve 100!
- Make multiple batches of a small amount. Don't just multiply ingredients in a huge industrial bowl and expect it to taste the way it does when you prepare it for your family of five.
- Be careful when serving trendy foods such as Mexican or Italian—you really need to know how to make a large quantity and still maintain authenticity.

Design a menu that will complement your garden setting while offering entrees and side dishes that can be easily made ahead of time, with minimal preparation.

THE MENU

*Oven Roasted Rosemary
    Chicken Breasts*
*Baked Ham with Mustards
    and Fruit Salsas*
Roasted Potato Salad
Vegetable Couscous Salad
*Strawberry Bread with
    Heart Butters*
*Miniature Muffins and
    Rolls with Herbed Butters*
Fruit Plate

Both the rosemary chicken breasts and the baked ham are popular supper entrees which lend themselves to advance preparation. The roasted potato salad contains no mayonnaise — a great choice for warm weather, and can also be prepared ahead of time along with the couscous salad. The breads and muffins can be baked weeks ahead and frozen. Simply thaw and serve. This entire menu can be served slightly chilled or at room temperature and is as delicious as it is easy!

Here are our step-by-step recipes to help you create this hearty and delightful garden meal. Either pass it along to your caterer or share it with family and friends . . . ENJOY!

COUSCOUS VEGETABLE SALAD

SALAD

Wilton Embossed Heart Pan

2½ cups water
1 (12 oz.) package (1¾ cups) plain, unseasoned couscous
1 medium red bell pepper, coarsely diced
1 medium green bell pepper, coarsely diced
1 can (14 oz.) artichoke hearts, drained and quartered
1 can (10 oz.) chick peas (garbanzo beans), drained
1 cup sliced green onions, including tops
½ sliced black olives, drained
½ cup thinly sliced celery

DRESSING

⅓ cup white balsamic or wine vinegar
⅔ cup olive oil
2 garlic cloves, pressed or chopped fine
2 tablespoons mint, chopped fine
salt and pepper to taste

To cook the couscous, bring water to a boil in medium saucepan. Stir in couscous, remove pan from heat, cover and let stand 5 minutes. Turn couscous into large mixing bowl and fluff with fork. Let stand 5 minutes, then fluff again. Mix in peppers, artichokes, chick peas, green onions, olives and celery. For dressing, whisk together oil, vinegar, garlic, mint, salt and pepper. Pour over couscous mixture and toss gently but thoroughly with a fork. Line pan with plastic wrap, press couscous mixture in pan. If making several salads, unmold each on serving tray, cover and refrigerate. If making one salad, cover and refrigerate in pan. Serve cold or at room temperature. *Serves 20 as part of a buffet.*

ROASTED NEW POTATO SALAD

Wilton 11 x 15 Sheet Pan

3 lbs. small red potatoes
½ cup olive oil
salt and pepper to taste
1 tablespoon fresh chopped dill
3 tablespoons dijon mustard
1 cup chopped celery
1 medium red onion, chopped

Preheat oven to 400°F. Clean and cut unpared potatoes into 3-4 slices. If potatoes are large, cut in half before slicing. Place in 11 x 15 pan. Toss with olive oil and roast 30-40 minutes or until potatoes are tender but still hold their shape. Stir every 10 minutes. When done, add seasonings and mustard while potatoes are still warm; stir. Cool one hour. Add celery and onion.

Toss to coat. Serve at room temperature. Can be refrigerated two days. If refrigerated, bring to room temperature before serving. *Serves 10 as part of a buffet.*

HERB OR FRUIT MOLDED BUTTER

*Wilton Mini Heart Pan or Hearts
    Candy Mold*

½ cup (1 stick) butter, softened
2 tablespoons fruit preserves or chopped fresh herbs—basil, tarragon, chives

Stir herbs or preserves into softened (not melted) butter. Press into Wilton Hearts Candy Mold or Mini Heart Pan. Freeze; remove from mold. Can be wrapped air tight and frozen for up to one week. Bring to room temperature before serving.

Makes 1 large mold (Mini Heart Pan) or 12-16 small molds (Candy Mold).

STRAWBERRY HEART BREAD

Wilton Heart Ring Pan

3 cups flour
1½ cups sugar
1 teaspoon baking soda
½ teaspoon salt
1 tablespoon cinnamon
2 packages (10 oz.) frozen strawberries, including juice
4 eggs
1¼ cup vegetable oil
1¼ cup nuts (walnuts or pecans)

Preheat oven to 350°F. Spray pan with vegetable pan spray. In large bowl, mix flour, sugar, baking soda, salt and cinnamon. Set aside. In a separate bowl combine strawberries with juice, eggs and oil. Pour strawberry mixture into flour and stir just until flour is absorbed. Stir in nuts. Pour into prepared pan and bake 50-60 minutes or until done (toothpick inserted in cake comes out clean). Cool. *Makes 10-12 servings.*

DRESSING THE BUFFET

Our buffet table is draped in a similar fashion as our guest tables. However, to maximize table space and to create an interesting tiered effect, our caterer has placed empty crates and boxes of varied heights to serve as the base of the buffet. The Wilton Garden Cake Stand is also used to conserve space and carry on the garden motif. The white bottom cloth is placed over the boxes and then the colorful raspberry overlay is draped on top. Be sure to count the number of serving pieces you will have on the buffet and create the appropriate number of tiers. You will then want to stage your buffet with empty serving dishes to determine where everything fits best. This is a lovely way to display your food and to gain space at the same time! Once our buffet has been set up our caterer wraps a sheer fabric in a winding fashion in and out of dishes and fills in spaces with colorful flowers from the garden. Looks good enough to eat!

THE CAKE

There is no dessert as special or as decadent as a wedding cake. So it only seems fitting to have your cake be a shining star on your wedding day.

To do this, your cake should stand alone on a separate table (in the shade, of course!) for all your guests to see. We have draped our table with a raspberry undercloth and then topped it with a very special heirloom cloth. Ivy is then wrapped at the base of the cake. The cake layers, which are separated by Wilton plates and lattice-look pillars, are accented with plumosa, ivy rubrum lilies, white iris, statice, and Queen Ann's lace, and topped with Wilton's Love's Duet Couple. A fresh floral nosegay can also serve as a cake topper and can be used as the bride's throw-away bouquet. Remember, too, that heat is not kind to most wedding cakes. Royal icing will hold up best, and buttercream and fondant will last much better than whipped cream icings. Consider your fillings, also. Custard and mousse fillings will not do as well in the heat as fruit fillings. The last thing you want is your caterer to be piecing together your wedding cake after it has collapsed from "heat exhaustion!"

CAUTION: When considering flowers or vines as decoration that may come in contact with food, be sure to consult your florist regarding toxicity. Silk flowers may be advised to substitute.

What makes a perfect garden cake? Flowers and more flowers! The cake itself needn't be elaborate—we've done one that's simply iced fluffy with a spatula. Your fresh flowers and greenery are what will make the cake seem to burst with color and life...just like your garden. The cakes that follow give you some good options for your garden setting.

THE BRIDAL BOUQUET

A cake for the purist at heart. Our scrolled cake stand holds three lighter-than-air tiers, each punctuated with glorious fresh flowers. This is an obvious choice for the garden reception, where floral beauty radiates from every detail. Easy to decorate and assemble, it's a time-saving option for those who like to "do it themselves". Serves 116.

ACCESSORIES YOU'LL NEED:

- 6, 10, 14 in. Round Pans
- 10, 14, 18 in. Separator Plates
- Meringue Powder
- Garden Cake Stand
- Cake Boards
- Small Angled Spatula
- Fluffy Boiled Icing *(3 recipes needed)*
- Fresh Flowers
- Ornament: *Together Forever Musical*

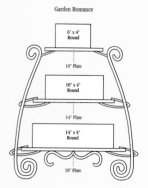

Garden Romance

Ice 2-layer cakes fluffy with angled spatula on separator plates. Use an ample amount of boiled icing on cakes. Fluff and swirl quickly. Boiled icing cannot be resmoothed or reworked like buttercream. Touching up after the initial icing will leave marks. At reception, position cakes on Garden Stand, add fresh flowers and wedding ornament.

FLUFFY BOILED ICING

3 Tablespoons Meringue Powder
½ cup cold water

Syrup:
2 cups granulated sugar
¼ cup corn syrup
½ cup water

Beat meringue powder and cold water until stiff, about 4 minutes. In a large microwave-safe measuring cup, stir sugar, corn syrup and water. In microwave oven, bring syrup mixture to boil (approximately 5 minutes). Remove when boiling stops. Slowly add syrup to meringue mixture while beating on low. Beat on HIGH for 4 minutes until stiff and glossy. YIELD: 8 cups.

For top of range: Mix sugar, corn syrup and water in 2 quart saucepan. Bring to a boil; cool slightly and follow directions above.

BELLS
IN HARMONY

Flowing ruffles and tolling bells create a sensation in crisp white. Ready-to-use fondant is an impeccable backdrop—and is a wonderful outdoor alternative to buttercream. Serves 156.

ACCESSORIES YOU'LL NEED:

- 8, 12, 16 in. Round Pans
- Tips 1, 2, 5, 349
- 3, 5 in. Lattice Pillars
  (1 pkg. each needed)
- 13 in. Lattice Pillars (6 needed)
- 10, 14, 18 in. Separator Plates
  (2 of each needed)
- Ruffle Pattern, p. 133
- Decorator Brush Set
- 1 in. Filigree Bells
  (2 pkgs. needed)
- Ready-To-Use Rolled Fondant
  (6 pkgs. needed)
- Gum Paste Mix (1 can needed)
- 30-Pc. Gum Paste Flowers Kit
- Cake Dividing Set
- Dowel Rods
- Buttercream Icing, p.118
- Fresh Flowers
- Ornament: *Love's Duet Couple, on Crystal-Look Base accented with ribbon.*

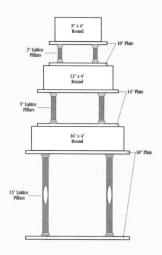

Prepare gum paste mix. Using instructions in gum paste flower book included in kit, make 70 forget me nots and 80 apple blossoms (omit wire). Pipe tip 1 dot centers for both flowers. Let dry.

Prepare 2-layer cakes for rolled fondant (p. 119) and pillar construction, see p. 113.

Divide 16 in. cake into 12ths, measure 2½ inches up from base of cake and mark. Pipe tip 5 beads around base of cake. Make ruffles by kneading together ¼ prepared gum paste and ¾ rolled fondant mixture. Cut 1 ruffle from pattern (p. 133) and ruffle the fondant following instructions on page 18 in gum paste book. Brush top edge of ruffle with water and press to position on cake. Cut and attach second ruffle slightly above the first. Shape and lift ruffles with pointed stick after attaching to cake. Position bells. Add gum paste flowers around garland with buttercream; add tip 349 leaves and tip 2 dots.

Divide 12 in. cake into 8ths, measure 2½ inches up from base of cake and mark. Pipe tip 5 beads around base of cake. Repeat same process for ruffles as with 16 in. cake. Pipe tip 2 beads along top edge of ruffle. Add tip 2 drop strings and dots. Position bells and gum paste flowers. Add tip 349 leaves.

Divide 8 in. cake into 6ths, measure 2½ inches up from base of cake and mark. Pipe tip 5 beads around base of cake. Repeat same process for ruffles as on previous cakes. Pipe tip 2 beads along top edge of ruffle. Add tip 2 drop strings and dots. Position gum paste flowers and add tip 349 leaves. Add tip 5 scallops around separator plates.

Note: To assemble ornament, attach Love's Duet Couple to Crystal-Look Base with hot glue gun. Gather lace ribbon around base and attach with hot glue. Make satin bow; attach to base with hot glue.

At reception: assemble cake; position fresh flowers and ornament.

LOVE'S IMPRESSION

A perfect pinnacle of fondant enrobed tiers. The colors are muted, echoed by the pretty patterned ribbon. Decorating is easy, using pattern presses and buttercream. Serves 306.

ACCESSORIES YOU'LL NEED:

- 8, 12, 16 in. Round Pans
- Tip 14
- Ivory*, Golden Yellow* Icing Colors
- Designer Pattern Press Set
- 8-Pc. Six Column Tier Set
- Dowel Rods
- Fresh Flower Holders (2 pkgs. needed)
- Flower Holder Ring
- Kolor-Flo Fountain
- Fanci-Foil Wrap
- Cake Dividing Set
- Ready-To-Use Rolled Fondant (12 pkgs. needed)
- Designer Bridesmaids, Pearlized Ivory (6 needed)
- Designer Groomsmen, Black Coat (6 needed)
- 1¾ in. wide ribbon (9 yards needed); styrofoam or wood block, fresh flowers
- Buttercream Icing, p. 118
- Ornament: *Garden Delight*

blend these colors to match ribbon

Prepare 7 2-layer 8 in. cakes, and 1 each 2-layer 12 and 16 in. cakes, for rolled fondant and pillar and stacked construction.

Cut fondant into strips ⅛ in. narrower than ribbon width. Lightly brush water on fondant, position around bottom edge of all tiers. Fondant strips are easiest to handle in 4 to 6 in. lengths. Position ribbon over fondant strips, securing at back of cake with dots of icing. Pipe tip 14 bottom shell borders.

Using Cake Dividing Set, divide 8 in. tiers into 4ths, 12 in. tier into 6ths, and 16 in. tier into 8ths. Imprint scroll pattern press on both sides of division marks. Using tip 14, outline imprints and add fleur-de-lis.

At reception, position 6 8 in. cakes in a circle, place wood or styrofoam block (measuring as tall as 8 in. tier and board) in center of cakes. Place 18 in. plate on top. Assemble fountain, position stacked tiers on pillars. Pipe tip 14 scallop around edge of plate. Arrange fresh flowers in holders and position ornament, bridesmaids and groomsmen.

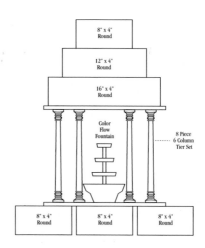

PERFECT POISE

This pure white design couldn't have more presence. Bold color flow and royal icing shapes stand out in relief on the bottom as two gently swaged tiers tower above. Serves 109.

ACCESSORIES YOU'LL NEED:

- 4-Pc. Oval Pan Set (All pans needed)
- Tips 2, 3, 199, 362, 363, 364
- 8½ x 6 in. and 11½ x 8½ in. Oval Separator Plates (1 each needed)
- Color Flow Mix
- Meringue Powder
- Hidden Pillars (2 pkgs. needed)
- White Tulle Circles (1 pkg. needed)
- Cake Boards
- Fanci-Foil Wrap
- Teardrops, Mini Teardrops, Circles and Fleurs de lis Patterns, p. 134
- Royal, Color Flow and Buttercream Icings, pgs. 118,119
- Fresh flowers
- Ornament: *Romantic Moments*

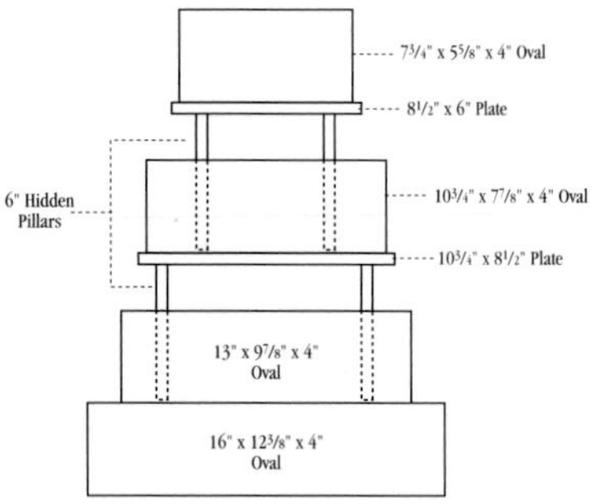

Using full-strength color flow (p. 119) and patterns, make 15 teardrops, 16 mini teardrops and 16 circles: Outline, then flow in centers of patterns. Let dry. Make extras to allow for breakage. When large teardrops are dry, turn over and attach tulle, trimmed to fit, with tip 2 line of royal icing. Let dry. Turn over and pipe tip 3 bead heart on tulle. Using royal icing, pipe tip 2 beads around each color flow piece. Let dry.

Using royal icing, pattern and waxed paper, pipe 16 fleurs de lis with tip 199 center shell and tip 364 "wings". Make extras to allow for breakage. Let dry.

Ice smooth 2-layer 7¾, 10¾ and 13 in. oval cakes and 1-layer 16 in. oval cake. Prepare for stacked and pillar construction.

On 7¾ in. oval: Mark cake at 2½ in. intervals. Mark scallops 1½ in. down from top. Pipe tip 3 triple drop strings at division marks, add tip 3 dots at end points. Pipe tip 199 crown top border with tip 3 dots. Add tip 363 shell bottom border.

On 10¾ in. oval: Mark cake at 2½ in. intervals. Mark scallops 1½ in. down from top. Pipe tip 362 zigzag garland. Overpipe with tip 3 drop strings; add tip 3 dots at garland points. Pipe tip 2 beads under garland. Pipe tip 199 crown top border with tip 3 dots. Add tip 363 shell bottom border.

On 13 in. oval: Pipe tip 199 crown top border with tip 3 dots. Add tip 363 shell bottom border. On 16 in. oval: Position large teardrops ½ in. from cake edge. Divide cake for drop strings at every 2½ in. mark on top edge. Pipe tip 3 double drop strings 1¼ in. deep. Add fleurs de lis on cake edge centered between large teardrops. Position color flow pieces, alternating circles and mini teardrops. Pipe tip 364 shell bottom border.

At reception, position cakes on hidden pillars, arrange fresh flowers and ornament.

6" Hidden Pillars

7¾" x 5⅝" x 4" Oval
8½" x 6" Plate
10¾" x 7⅞" x 4" Oval
10¾" x 8½" Plate
13" x 9⅞" x 4" Oval
16" x 12⅝" x 4" Oval

GLITTER
AND GRANDEUR

Pull out all the stops! This cake has the proper wedding day dazzle, with sparkling leaves of silver and gold—plus a towering shape, built upon our tall crystal-look pillars and staircases. Serves 209.

ACCESSORIES YOU'LL NEED:

- 9 in., 15 in. Petal Pans
- 18 in. Half Round Pan (3 in. deep)
- Tips 3, 4, 6, 10, 12, 101, 102, 103, 104, 362, 364
- Flower Nail No. 7
- Meringue Powder
- 6mm Pearl Beading* (4 pkgs. needed)
- Crystal Stairways (2 needed)
- Plastic Dowel Rods
- 7 in. Crystal-Look Pillars (4 needed)
- 13¾ in. Crystal-Look Pillars (4 needed)
- 9 in. Crystal-Look Plates (2 needed)
- 17 in. Crystal-Look Plates (2 needed)
- 1¼ in. Gold Leaves (1 pkg. needed)
- 1¼ in. Silver Leaves (1 pkg. needed)
- Mini Floral Lights
- Designer Groomsmen, Black Tux (3 needed)
- Designer Bridesmaids, Black Dress (3 needed)
- Royal, Buttercream Icings, p. 118
- Fresh Flowers
- Crystal Look Bowl
- Ornament: *Dedication*

Make royal icing roses: Thirty tip 101 with tip 4 bases; forty tip 102 with tip 6 bases; forty tip 103 with tip 10 bases; sixty tip 104 with tip 12 bases. Make extras to allow for breakage and let dry.

Ice two 2-layer 9 in. and one 2-layer 15 in. petal tiers for pillar construction. Prepare four 18 in. half rounds, 2 in. each, in two layers; ice and prepare for pillar construction.

9 in. Petal (top tier): Position 4 rows of pearl beading around base. Pipe tip 3 elongated double drop strings, 2 in. wide and 3 in. deep, centered on each petal division. Pipe tip 362 top and bottom shell borders. Position tip 103, 102, 101 roses; attach leaves with dots of icing.

15 in. Petal: Position 4 rows of pearl beading around base. Mark center of each petal, and pipe tip 3 triple drop strings 2 in. wide and 1½ in. deep to right of center mark. Pipe tip 362 top and bottom shell borders. Position tip 104, 103, 102, 101 roses; attach leaves with dots of icing.

18 in. Round: Position 4 rows of pearl beading around base. Pipe tip 364 bottom shell border. Pipe tip triple drop strings 3 in. wide and 1½ in. deep, leaving ½ in. between sections. Mark one section on each side of tier for placement of stairways (see p. 114). Position tip 104, 103, 102 roses; attach leaves with dots of icing.

9 in. Petal (positioned on 18 in.): Position four rows of pearl beading around base. Pipe tip 3 triple drop strings, 1½ in. deep, on each petal division. Add tip 362 top shell border.

At reception: Assemble tiers on pillars; arrange flowers in crystal bowls. Position mini floral lights in ornament; position ornament on cake. Position stairways, bridesmaids and groomsmen.

Remove pearls before cutting and serving.

9" x 4" Petal
9" Plate
7" Crystal Look Pillars
9" Plate
15" x 4" Petal
17" Plate
13¾" Crystal Look Pillars
9" x 4" Petal
17" Plate
18" x 4" Round

BLISSFUL PAIR

A lighter touch that will charm everyone. Our joyous couple poses beneath a garden gazebo bedecked with blossoms and cornelli lace. Soft yellow, green and violet icings are ideal for a springtime celebration. Serves 128 if saving half-ball cake for first anniversary. • Serves 122 if saving 8 in. round cake for first anniversary.

ACCESSORIES YOU'LL NEED:

- 8, 12, 14, 16 in. Round Pans
- Ball Pan (½ of pan is used)
- Tips 2, 5, 16, 18, 103, 104, 224, 225, 233, 352
- Pink, Lemon Yellow, Royal Blue, Willow Green, Violet Icing Colors
- Decorating Comb
- Gazebo Cake Kit
- Small Doves (2 needed)
- Cake Boards
- Meringue Powder
- 10 in. Separator Plates (2 needed)
- 6½ in. Arched Pillars (1 pkg. needed)
- 18 in. Ruffle Board®
- Cake Dividing Set
- Decorator Brush Set
- Buttercream, Royal Icings, p. 118
- Ornament: *Petite Together Forever Couple*

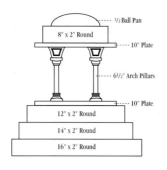

½ Ball Pan
8" x 2" Round
10" Plate
6½" Arch Pillars
10" Plate
12" x 2" Round
14" x 2" Round
16" x 2" Round

Using royal icing, make drop flowers—150 each color (tip 224 pink, tip 224 blue, tip 225 lemon yellow, tip 225 violet) with tip 2 dot centers. Let dry.

Using tip 103 and royal icing, pipe loop portions of 8 bows. Pipe flowing tails of bows separately. Let dry.

Using thinned down royal icing and decorator brush, cover 2 doves with icing. Let dry on waxed paper.

Ice smooth 1-layer 8 in., 12 in., 14 in., 16 in. cakes and half-ball cake. Prepare for stacked and pillar construction.

Stack half-ball on 8 in. round; divide into 8ths and mark garland ¾ in. down from top edge of 8 in. cake. Pipe tip 2 cornelli lace on ball and down over edge of cake to garland. Pipe tip 5 beads from top center of half ball down to 8 in. cake at division marks. Pipe tip 16 zigzag garland. Pipe tip 18 shell bottom border. Position flowers on garland mark and top of ball cakes. Pipe tip 2 drop strings; add tip 352 leaves.

Divide 12 in. cake into 8ths and mark ¾ in. down for garland. Pipe tip 18 bottom shell border. Pipe tip 16 string garland between division marks. Attach flowers to garlands, add tip 352 leaves. Add tip 233 pull-out grass around separator plate. Pipe tip 16 top shell border. Attach bow pieces with dots of icing.

Divide 14 in. cake into 12ths, mark garlands ¾ in. down from top edge. Pipe tip 18 bottom shell border. Pipe tip 16 string garland between division marks; attach flowers to garlands and add tip 352 leaves. Pipe tip 16 top shell border.

Divide 16 in. cake into 12ths and mark garlands ¾ in. down from top edge. Use decorating comb to make a swag drapery effect. Pipe tip 18 bottom shell border. Pipe tip 104 ruffle above bottom shell border. Pipe tip 16 top shell border. Attach flowers above ruffle; add tip 352 leaves.

At reception, assemble cake and gazebo (small sections only). Attach doves to pillars using royal icing. Position ornament.

CANDLELIT ROMANCE

Wire lace and candlelight make this cake a romantic, climactic event.
The openwork accessories set a fanciful mood, ideally suited to icing flowers and greenery.
Our candlelight stand provides effortless assembly. Serves 122.

ACCESSORIES YOU'LL NEED:

- 7 in. Round Pan
- 12, 15 in. Hexagon Pans
- Tips 5, 6, 7, 8, 9, 11, 102, 103, 104, 349
- Leaf Green, Rose Icing Colors
- Candlelight Cake Stand
- Cake Dividing Set
- 14 in. Separator Plate
- Meringue Powder
- Wooden Dowel Rods
- 4 x 4 in. Filigree Heart Frames (2 pkgs. needed)
- 8 in. Plates (2 needed) from Crystal-Clear Cake Divider Set
- Wire Lace Separator
- Cake Boards, Fanci Foil Wrap
- Floral Puff Accent (4 needed)
- Taper Candles (4 needed)
- Buttercream, Royal Icings, p. 118
- Ornament: *Sweetness*

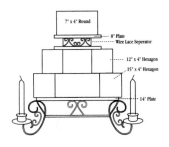

Using royal icing, make 360 tip 102 sweet peas (120 each: light rose, medium rose, dark rose). Make 300 tip 103 sweet peas (100 each: light rose, medium rose, dark rose). Make 300 tip 104 sweet peas (100 each: light rose, medium rose, dark rose). Make extras to allow for breakage. Let dry.

Ice and prepare 2-layer cakes for stacked construction. Cut a board large enough to fit 15 in. hexagon cake and cover with foil. Divide 7 in. round into 6ths. Arrange tip 102 sweet peas around top border and cascade flowers down sides of cake; add tip 349 leaves.

For 12 in. hexagon: Pipe tip 9 line around base of cake; add tip 6 triple bead bottom border. Position 8 in. plate on top of cake; edge plate with tip 5 beads. Pipe tip 8 zigzag-motion mound of icing at corners in a triangle shape. Position tip 103 sweet peas into icing, cascading flowers down corners of cake. Pipe tip 349 leaves.

For 15 in. hexagon: Pipe tip 11 line of icing around bottom border of cake. Pipe tip 7 triple bead bottom border. Pipe tip 8 zigzag-motion mound of icing at corners in a triangle shape. Position tip 103 and 104 sweet peas into icing, cascading flowers down corners of cake. Pipe tip 349 leaves. Attach filigree hearts to top, using buttercream icing.

At reception: Position separator plate on stand, then place cake. Place wire separator on top of 12 in. hexagon. Trim center flower and pearl spray from floral puff accent; attach to plate legs with icing. Position 7 in. round cake and pipe tip 8 line of icing around bottom edge. Add tip 5 triple bead bottom border. Position ornament and candles.

THE
AT-HOME
RECEPTION

"Home is Where the Heart is." This well-known

sentiment is often the inspiration behind many couples'

decision to celebrate their marriage in a very special place—

at home.   Whether you choose your own home, or the

home of family or friends, the intimacy, warmth and

tradition that prevails in a home setting is unmatched

by any other. For many brides, especially those who have

lived their whole lives in one house, it seems only natural

to celebrate such a momentous occasion in a place that

holds so much meaning and joy.   And in many instances,

a reception at home provides you with optimal

freedom and control over every wedding detail.

Nothing is more personal
for family and friends than a wedding
reception at home

BENEFITS TO AN AT-HOME RECEPTION

Aside from the sentimental advantages, there are many other practical benefits to having a reception at home. At-Home receptions, in general, are less expensive than formal dinner receptions and are perfect for second weddings, "late-in-life" weddings or weddings where there is not an extensive guest list or budget. All in all, the at-home reception can be a less extravagant option and is typically more manageable than the formal hotel or banquet hall reception. Many components of a larger reception, such as dinner menus, seating, music, etc. are limited, making your job of planning a little bit easier. It is the perfect choice for the couple who prefers to keep things simple.

TRANSFORMING YOUR HOME

Despite the many advantages of an at-home reception, there are many unique, not-so-simple tasks to undertake before you can turn your home into a reception hall. Attention to detail will be critical to the success of your at-home reception. Be sure to think through all that's involved. The job you have ahead is not always easy; be prepared for some disruptions on the home front as you prepare for your day.

Before deciding on a reception at home, consider these questions:

Is your home big enough? Be realistic when it comes to space. Remember, you will need places for food, beverages, parking, coats, gifts, food preparation, kitchen staff, desserts, wedding cake, seating, plus your guests!

Is your home in the condition it needs to be in? If you have unfinished construction or remodeling projects, can they be done in time for the wedding?

This is a good time to prepare your home for guests by painting rooms, hanging new window treatments, cleaning clutter, or fixing that lampshade that never looked just right.

Does your home decor complement your wedding style? If your dress, colors, invitations etc. reflect a Victorian or romantic style, a contemporary home with modern furnishings would not be appropriate.

Are you willing to move out furniture to create space for your guests? If so, where will it go?

Are you willing to have your home in a state of chaos for a number of months? You may be visited by caterers and florists as you plan the wedding reception, and the phone calls will be numerous. Can your home life withstand the temporary disruptions? These are all things that you or your homeowner must be prepared for when planning a wedding at home.

The results are well worth it . . . but not without a price!

PLANNING YOUR AT-HOME RECEPTION

You have considered all of the benefits and pitfalls of having your wedding at home and you have decided that this is what you and your groom want. Now the planning begins. As with any wedding, you must first decide on your guest list so you know the number of guests to serve. Once you know this you can begin planning your menu, traffic patterns, layout and other details of the event.

You should also carefully consider how much of the planning and execution of the event you want to take on yourself, versus how much should be handled by a professional wedding planner and/or caterer. Some brides, who have many local family members and friends, can comfortably handle everything from the invitations to the food—right down to the flowers. You, on the other hand, may feel more comfortable delegating some of the responsibility to professionals—especially when it comes to menu planning, food preparation, clean-up, and flowers.

Just remember one important rule of thumb—be realistic in determining what you can handle, and take on no more. This will help reduce any unnecessary stress and will make your at-home planning experience a positive one.

STYLE AND THEME

Once again, style ranks high as a primary consideration before planning your reception. For our at-home reception, we have chosen a rustic, yet classic English Tudor home. The heavy woodwork and bay windows in this charming cottage create a theme that is soft, warm and romantic. To help enhance these feelings, flower choices and colors are muted in light tones of pink, yellow, blue and lavender. Many of the home's rich fabrics and furnishings will remain intact for the reception and antique serving pieces featured at the buffet are borrowed from family and friends. All of these details help create a setting that is both meaningful and inviting.

STAFFING

Whether you hire a professional caterer, or simply enlist the help of family and friends, you will need a number of people to work your many "stations." Here is a list that will help

you plan out your staffing needs. (based on the reception featured here)

1 greeter with champagne
2 coat takers
1–2 coat room attendants
1 restroom attendant
1 gift attendant
1 bartender
1 music attendant
4–6 bus people
2–4 valet attendants
4–6 kitchen staff
4–6 clean-up

WHEN SPACE IS TIGHT

Here are a few ideas to help create a little more space if you can just cut down that guest list.

• Stagger your guests. Have guests come at different times, as with an open house. This means your guests will be coming and going throughout the evening and not everyone will be there at the same time. Beware, this can make food planning more difficult.

• Have hors d'oeuvres passed instead of taking up space at a buffet table. Although this will add to your staffing requirements, it may give you a whole extra room for guests.

• Remove as much furniture as possible—even in bedrooms.

• If the season and weather condi-

tions are mild, move guests outside to a deck area or add a tent. (See p. 17 of the Garden Reception section for ideas on outdoor receptions)

A FEW WORDS OF ADVICE

• Be sure to inquire about insurance, especially if you're serving alcohol. Be prepared to make alternative transportation arrangements for guests who have too much to drink. Know your liabilities as the homeowner, and know what to do if someone gets injured on your property. Also, make sure you see your caterer's certificate of insurance and inquire about blanket coverage.

• Don't mix toxic flowers with anything edible. Consult your florist.

• If children are invited to your reception, you should consider a separate menu and a play area. You might even hire a baby-sitter for the evening so parents can enjoy themselves knowing their children are well cared for. Also, make sure children do not wander outside or near cars without adult supervision.

• If your home is located in a rural area, include maps in your invitations and post signs or balloons along the way.

• Have plenty of ice—especially if it's hot.

• Don't forget about other concerns, such as out-of-town guest accommodations, rehearsals, transportation, videographer and photographer. Make sure your photographer captures the "at-home feeling" you've worked so hard to achieve.

• Be sure to get the appropriate permission if you plan to use nearby church or retail parking.

• Don't try to change too much about your home. Keep as many things intact as possible, that's the reason you chose this as your reception setting to begin with!

TIME OF DAY

Our at-home reception will be held in the evening—after 8:00 p.m. However, there are many other reception options which will be defined by time of day and menu. For instance, a mid-day brunch or lunch reception is perfect for an at-home event. Or, why not let the sun be your guide? A "sunrise" at-home wedding, followed by a breakfast celebration, is a refreshing and unique idea. If a room in your home has a western exposure with a particularly wonderful view, then an evening "sunset" reception followed by cocktails and hors d'oeuvres is also a lovely option. Another "sweet" idea is to have a lavish dessert reception where you and your guests indulge in every decadent cake, tort, cookie and pastry you can imagine. This has a great visual appeal and is perfect for the reception in the late evening or as the clock strikes midnight on New Year's Eve! Just remember, your possibilities are endless and when you choose your time of day, you are also choosing the mood.

SELECTING YOUR MENU

In most cases, your home will accommodate standing room only for your guests. Unless you have a very large home with many large rooms, you will not be seating your guests for a full meal. Therefore, most at-home receptions feature a menu consisting of hors d'oeuvres and "finger" food only. If many of your guests are family members, you may want to include a traditional family dish that everyone will enjoy. The most important thing to remember when designing your menu, however, aside from serving the best quality food you can afford, is to make sure the food is easy to eat. Your menu choices should not require flatware and should be consumed in one or two bites. Your guests should

be able to stand and eat comfortably and without feeling awkward.

As we mentioned earlier, time of day has a lot to do with setting the mood and creating the overall reception theme. It also will help dictate your menu. One of the reasons we chose an evening reception—after 8:00 p.m.—was to keep our menu from getting too heavy. Your wedding budget may also be a consideration. If your reception hours fall between 6:00 and 8:00 p.m., then the appropriate menu should feature a heavy buffet. Mid to late afternoon receptions, as with an evening reception, can offer much lighter fare. You may think that creating a "heavy" buffet is a whole separate undertaking, but actually it is very simple. Your caterer should have plenty of menu ideas; however, if you're preparing the food yourself, a few simple additions will do the trick. Just add a carved meat option, such as beef tenderloin or smoked turkey, to make the buffet a little more substantial for your hungry guests. You can serve it sliced with an assortment of miniature bakery rolls, or, for a more dramatic effect, you can have a chef carving the selection at the head of the buffet.

Since you or your catering staff will be working in a "family" kitchen, as opposed to a large restaurant-sized kitchen, make sure that the food is cooked and prepared in advance, and requires very little re-heating or assembly. Try to include foods that can be served cold or at room temperature. This not only makes preparation easier, but these foods will also hold up

longer on a buffet table that may be out several hours. Food trays should be re-filled continually and garnishes should be freshened. And as always, be sure to practice safe food handling and cooking techniques. Anything with meat or eggs must be cooked thoroughly and served at the appropriate temperature. Avoid serving foods that have a tendency to spoil. (See p. 22 of the Garden Wedding for more ideas on safe food choices.) Also, depending on the size of your kitchen and the number of people you are serving, you may want to create an extra area for food preparation that is out of sight, such as a garage, or screened-in porch.

In addition to your main hors d'oeuvres menu, you might also consider having a separate dessert buffet with your wedding cake as the highlight. This can be set up after the main buffet or concurrently in a separate room. Bite-size pastries, petit fours and handmade chocolates are good choices since they are lovely to look at and easy to eat while standing.

AT-HOME RECEPTION MENU

For 80-100 guests:

Champagne, Punch, Wine
Chilled Shrimp on Ice
Meatballs
Quiche
Fruit Kabobs
Vegetable Platter & Dip
Cheese & Fruit Tray
Pate, in Braided Bread
Smoked Turkey and Chutney on
  Miniature Buns
Crab Tarts
Wedding Cake
Fruit Tarts, Candies,
Nuts
Chocolate Mousse Bites
Coffee & Tea

Most "At-Home" receptions feature
a menu consisting of hors d'oeuvres and
"finger" food only.

THE WEDDING CAKE

Whether your reception is a grand scale event at a hotel ballroom, or an intimate gathering of family and friends, one element remains the same—your wedding cake. In keeping with our theme of classic romance, this cake speaks for itself. We start with a three-tiered wire cake stand and a Wilton's charming Kissing Love Birds ornament, both which have been painted to create an antique effect.*

The cake is made up of three stacked fondant covered tiers decorated with rolled fondant flowers that have been cut with small flower cutters. Each flower contains a blue icing center. A small shell icing border is added and then satin ribbon and bows are delicately wrapped around the bottom of the cake for the perfect finishing touch.

NOTE: When painting any cake decorations, be sure they DO NOT come in contact with the cake. In this case, the ornament has been placed on a separate piece of fondant that will not be consumed by guests.

The dining room's bay window serves as the perfect spot to showcase our wedding cake. A light and airy garland frames the window and table featuring springarie, ruscus and blue delphinium. We have also filled some family heirlooms with finger desserts and candies and then accented the sweets with soft, romantic flowers and colorful sheer fabric. The candlelight also contributes to the soft romantic effect. In combination, these elements create a dessert station that is almost too pretty to eat!

BAR & BEVERAGES

When it comes to deciding what liquor, if any, is served to your guests, the options are about as limitless as your food menu. Once again, however, an at-home event should be as streamlined as possible. You may not have the space or the budget to set up a complete open bar, so here are a few ideas. As guests arrive at the front entrance, they will be greeted and handed a glass of champagne. In the living room, where most of the guests will be gathering, a small bar has been set up for punch, wine and any other non-alcoholic beverages. Guests can serve themselves, or you may want to hire a bartender to serve guests and maintain the bar area. The punch table has been draped with family linens and embellished with mesh ribbon and sand drift lilies.

When setting up your bar, be sure to keep enough champagne and white wine chilled. You will also want to protect the floor below your bar station with heavy plastic liners, especially underneath coolers which may leak. If you are courageous enough to serve red wine, be sure to move any upholstered furniture or expensive rugs that may get spilled on. Your bartender should have clean towels on hand to wipe up any drips and spills quickly. You will also want to choose the appropriate stemware for the drinks you are serving. Try to choose a glass style that is multi-functional in order to limit the total number of glasses you will need at the bar. You should also plan on 2.5 glasses per guest so that you or your caterer is not having to wash glasses. It is also a good idea to have someone on your caterer's staff assigned to clearing all empty glassware throughout the evening.

If you choose not to serve alcohol, there are a great number of beverages you can serve your guests, including sparkling waters, non-alcoholic champagnes, wines and beers, mulled ciders, soft drinks, fresh juices, coffee, herbal teas and punches galore! You may also want to include some of these options to supplement your alcoholic beverage selection for those who cannot or prefer not to drink alcohol. Whether or not you serve alcohol, a coffee station should be set up in conjunction with the wedding cake and dessert.

TRAFFIC FLOW & OTHER PLANNING CONSIDERATIONS

Depending on the layout and size of your home, you will need to decide "what will be where?" and "who will be where?" Here are the main areas for which you will have to plan.

Kitchen: Your kitchen is most certainly put to the test when you have an at-home reception. Clear out as many of your personal things as you can, especially from your refrigerator and freezer. Create as much counter space as possible for food assembly. And don't forget about adding extra food prep areas in the garage or porch, if possible. If using disposable serveware, be sure to have extra garbage dumpsters for dirty glassware and dishes in a place that is out of sight from your guests. You should also do whatever you can to separate the kitchen area from your guests—but be sure your serving staff has easy access in and out. Portable accordion screens do a nice job and can be decorated with ribbons or fresh flowers.

Parking: You will probably have to count on street parking and neighbors' driveways, with permission, for guest parking, unless your home is conveniently located next to a church or retail parking facility. Be sure to call your local police to inquire about permits and tell them how many cars you will be expecting. They may be able to

re-route or direct neighborhood traffic for your event. As a polite gesture to neighbors, you should forewarn them of your event so they are not taken by surprise. Some may generously offer their driveways for additional parking. You might also consider having a valet service park the cars for your guests. Weather conditions will also play a part in the parking decisions. Last but not least, be sure to have someone directing guests in their cars while backing out of difficult situations and to be on the lookout if there will be children in attendance.

Guest Entry: This is where your guests will be greeted. Coats and gifts should be taken as guests arrive. A spare bedroom or den can serve as a coat room and can be handled similarly to coat checks at restaurants. Racks and hangers should be set up since many people will be wearing very fine coats, hats, even furs, depending on the time of year. The gifts should be in a room that is secure or if you have the space, you can have a separate gift table in your living room, dining room, or entryway.

Dining Room: This should serve as your buffet and dessert area. Guests should be able to make their way around the buffet table comfortably. They may also congregate here, so it is a good idea to remove any unnecessary furniture. Make sure there is enough room near the wedding cake for you and your groom to cut it and for the photographer who will want to capture that moment on film.

Living Room: In addition to your dining room, this is where your guests are most likely to mingle and it is where you may choose to set up your bar area. We have made this room especially inviting with a warm, cozy fire in the fireplace and a romantic floral spray draping the mantle. Although most of the guests will be standing, we have created some limited cluster seating to accommodate the elderly, or people with special needs. Once again, you will want to remove any unnecessary furniture that will obstruct the flow of traffic.

Music: In most cases, an at-home wedding will not allow you to have a full orchestra or band. You may, however, want to have a small area set aside for a DJ or an instrumentalist, such as a flutist, guitarist, or violinist. If you have a piano, you might hire someone professionally or from a local church to play for your guests. Pre-taped music can also be piped in through stereo speakers, but you will have to assign this task to someone who can be responsible for making sure the music is continuous and at the right volume. This is especially critical if you are conducting your ceremony at home, also.

Restroom: Although you would think a restroom is something you don't need to give a whole lot of attention to, it should still look special and tie into the rest of your wedding theme. After all, it's safe to say that all of your guests will visit it at one time or another throughout the evening. We have made sure that our guests' journey up the staircase to the restroom is a pleasant one. We adorned the railing with beautiful swaged ribbons and flower clusters that are consistent with flowers used throughout the rest of the house. Before making the final turn onto the stairs leading to the restroom, old family pictures in antique frames are displayed on top of a built-in wooden cabinet at the landing. The restroom itself has been impeccably cleaned and all personal items have been removed. The sink area is accented with a fresh flower spray and nosegay and a neat stack of engraved paper napkins are made available for guests to dry their hands. Decorative soaps, potpourri and candles are wonderful accessories and the perfect way to keep the restroom smelling sweet and fresh. The restroom will require maintenance quite regularly to replenish towels and toilet paper, to empty garbage and to wipe up any mess around the sink. (Note: A downstairs restroom is best to accommodate elderly guests.)

Bride's Room: If space allows, you should make sure the wedding party has a separate room for their personal belongings, along with a private restroom. This is also a good place to keep honeymoon luggage.

EXTERIOR DECOR

Aside from the many decorative details we have outlined throughout the inside of the house, there are a few we should mention for the outside. As your guests pull up to your home, you want them to get a feeling that is unique to your wedding. The exterior decor should let people know that something very special is happening inside. As you review the many options for the outside, consider the architecture of your home and consult your florist for ideas. Of course, general landscaping should look its best, but in addition to a well manicured yard and garden, we have added a few special touches. Two double-balled topiaries featuring lilies, gardenias, delphinium and iris stand nearly six feet tall at each side of the stone archway which greets our guests. Small votive candles are placed along the walkway illuminating the path to the front door. And perhaps most stunning of all, a strong mix of lilies, snapdragons, hydrangea, and roses create identical cascading waterfalls at each side of the doorway as guests enter the home. Keep in mind that unlike the interior, where your flowers should be in proportion to each room without overpowering it, the exterior invites you to get as much color and impact for your money as possible. Choose large, bold blooms that will be seen from a distance.

From guest entry to stairways to restrooms, each area of the home should look special and tie into your wedding theme.

INTERLUDE

A candlelit spectacular, brimming over with flowers. Don't be dissuaded by the volume of blooms—these are fondant flowers, which allow you to turn out the 500 roses and daisies required in far less time than piped icing flowers would take. Serves 71.

ACCESSORIES YOU'LL NEED:

- 6, 12 in. Round Pans
- 8 in. (3 in. deep) Pan
- Tips 2, 16
- Cornflower Blue Icing Color
- Candlelight Cake Stand
- 14 in. separator plate (from Crystal-Clear Cake Divider set).
- Ready To Use Rolled Fondant (3 pkgs. needed)
- Cake Dividing Set
- 30 Pc. Gum Paste Flowers Kit
- 6 yards ⅜ in. ribbon
- 4 taper candles
- Buttercream Icing, p. 118
- Ornament: *Kissing Love Birds*

Make 510 flowers from rolled fondant using calyx, wild rose and small daisy cutters from Gum Paste Kit (170 each size). After each flower is cut, place on thick piece of foam and press in center of flower firmly with #2 stick from kit to form a cup shape. Using buttercream, add tip 2 dot centers. Let dry.

Make 10 ribbon bows: Cut a 12 in. piece of ribbon for each bow. Loop both ends, then tie a shoelace-type bow. Set aside.

Bake 2-layer 6 in. cake, each layer 1½ in. Bake 2-layer 12 in. cake. Bake 1-layer 8 in. cake, 3 in. high.

Prepare cakes for rolled fondant (p. 119) and stacked construction.

For 6 in. and 8 in. cakes, pipe tip 16 shell bottom border. Attach flowers with buttercream icing. Divide bottom cake into 10ths. Add tip 16 shell bottom border. Cut a piece of ribbon the circumference of 12 in. cake. Position ribbon around center of cake and attach bows at each division, using buttercream icing. Attach flowers with buttercream icing.

At reception: Place cake on stand. Position ornament and candles.

Note: Ornament and stand may be spray painted silver. If paintng ornament, place on a fondant-covered cardboard circle to protect cake.

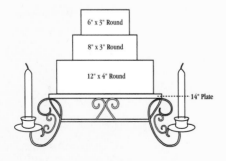

DANCING ON AIR

*Perfect for serving a smaller crowd, this single-tier cake is as breathtaking as any
multi-tiered design. Its rolled fondant surface holds up well in warmer weather—an ideal
choice for an intimate garden reception. Serves 77.*

ACCESSORIES YOU'LL NEED:

- 14 in. Round Pan
- Tips 2, 5
- Orange, Pink, Willow Green Icing Colors
- Letters Pattern (see p. 124)
- Ready-To-Use Rolled Fondant (3 pkgs. needed)
- Color Flow Mix
- Gum Paste Mix
- Gum Paste Flowers Kit
- Cake Board
- Flower Formers
- Decorator Brush Set
- Cake Dividing Set
- Buttercream Icing, p. 128
- Non-toxic pastel chalks
- Ornament: *First Dance Couple*

14" x 4"
Round

Following instructions in Gum Paste Flowers Book, make roses with toothpicks instead of wire. Prepare gum paste mix, make coral gum paste roses: 30 with 2 rows of petals and 6 with 1 row of petals. Cut out leaves, shape and dry on flower formers. Let dry.

To color flowers, grate pink and orange chalk with a tea strainer. Mix colors to reach a coral shade and brush on flowers with decorator brushes. Set aside. Save remaining chalk for garlands.

To make monogram letters: Place waxed paper over pattern and outline with tip 2 and full-strength color flow icing, p. 119. Let set. Flow in with thinned color flow and tip 2 to fill in letter. Let dry. Make extras to allow for breakage.

Make 2 bow loops (on top of cake) with 4 in. x 6 in. pieces of fondant. Fold pieces in half and pinch ends together. Make 2 streamers with 3 in. x 5 in. pieces of fondant; cut tails into a "V" shape; pinch opposite end together. Let set overnight.

Prepare and cover 2-layer 14 in. cake with 2 packages of rolled fondant. Divide cake into 10ths. Mark 5 sections on cake for fondant garlands, beginning at top edge and gradually lowering mark 1 inch each time. Repeat process going upward on cake for back garlands. Pipe tip 5 bead bottom border.

To make garland drapes, cut each piece of fondant to measure 6 in. x 9 in. Make three pleats and pinch at both ends. Attach to sides of cake with water. Dust garland, bows and streamers with brush and grated chalk. Position leaves and flowers at each garland point.

At reception, position ornament, letters, bows and streamers on top of cake. Add a few random roses on top.

LOVE BIRDS

Curving borders, abundant floral bouquets and distinctive ornamentation characterize the Philippine Method of Decorating. Although intricately detailed in many ways, Ready-To-Use Rolled Fondant Icing and make-ahead embellishments save you crucial time during wedding week. Serves 128, saving both oval tiers for the first anniversary.

ACCESSORIES YOU'LL NEED:

- 16 in. Square Pan
- Oval Pan Set (7¾ x 5⅝ in. used)
- Tips 1A, 2, 5, 12, 13, 18, 21, 45, 65, 66, 67
- Royal Blue Icing Color
- Panoramic Egg Kit
- Plastic Dowel Rods
- Ready-To-Use Rolled Fondant (5 pkgs. needed)
- Bomboniere!® White Tulle Circles (2 pkgs. needed)
- Cake Boards, Fanci-Foil Wrap, Tuk-N-Ruffle
- Meringue Powder
- 9 in. Crystal-Look Spiked Pillars (3 sets needed)
- Flower Spikes (2 pkgs. needed)
- 8½ x 6 in. Oval Separator Plates (2 needed)
- Filigree Swirls
- Florist Wire
- Swan Pattern (p. 125)
- Royal, Buttercream Icings, p. 118
- Granulated sugar, white florist tape, white curling ribbon, sponge, styrofoam block, hot glue gun
- Ornament: *Promise*

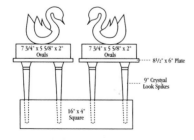

Prepare two swans several days in advance; make extras to allow for breakage: Following instructions in Panoramic Egg Kit, make solid sugar half egg using top half of large egg mold. While mold is wet, cut a slit ½ in. wide x ⅜ in. deep in wider end of egg to

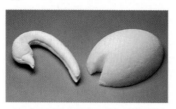

insert neck. Let dry. Pipe swan head/neck using royal icing, tip 1A and pattern; add tip 12 beak. Let dry overnight, carefully turn over and overpipe; let dry. Pull out with tip 1A on back (narrow end) of sugar mold for tail. When pieces are completely dry, smooth over seams with royal icing, let dry. Thin royal icing with water and paint pieces smooth. Let dry completely. Using hot glue gun, attach head/neck and two filigree swirls for wings to sugar form, let set. Decorate swan with royal icing, beginning at tail and working toward head. Pipe tip 67 pull-out leaves to cover tail, back and wings; at base of neck begin using tip 66, at top of neck change to tip 65 and finish head. Add tip 2 pull out dot eyes. Let dry completely.

Pipe flowers on wires using royal icing as follows: Make approximately 75 tip 45 rosebuds with tip 5 pistils on 4 in. wire lengths; some solid blue and the remaining spatula striped blue and white. Make approximately 80 tip 13 sampaquita sprays; 40 on 4 in. wires and 40 on 12 in. wires: Use tip 13 and pipe stars directly on wires. Start at the tip of the wire and pipe stars at ½ in. intervals. Insert wire end into styrofoam block to dry. Make extras of all flowers to allow for breakage and let dry.

Make 32 tulle puffs: Gather a tulle circle at center, twist on 6 in. wire. Make 40 tendrils: Cover 6 in. wire length with florist tape, wrap around wooden dowel rod or pencil, slide off. Make 35 ribbon loops: Gather 26 in. length curling ribbon into 3 loops with tails, twist on 6 in. wire.

Assemble floral bouquets: Arrange components and wrap ends with florist tape, set into flower spike. Make 4 large bouquets; for each use 11 rosebuds, 6 short sampaquita sprays, 3 tulle puffs, 5 tendrils and 5 ribbon loops. Make 4 small bouquets; for each use 7 rosebuds, 4 short sampaquita sprays, 2 tulle puffs, 4 tendrils, 3 ribbon loops. Make floral bouquet for positioning behind swans using 35 tall sampaquita sprays, 2 ribbon loops, 3 tendrils and 3 tulle puffs. Wrap ends in florist tape and place in 9 in. spiked pillar. Set all aside.

Cover two 1-layer ovals and 2-layer square with buttercream icing. Dowel rod ovals where swans will be positioned and prepare square for push-in pillar construction. Cover tiers with rolled fondant (use 4 pkgs. to cover 16 in. square). Cut two cake boards sized to fit bottom of swans, cover with rolled fondant.

Using a small sponge, dab thinned royal icing on sides of tiers and covering ovals. Pipe bottom borders: Tip 21 shells on 16 in. tier and tip 18 "C" motion shells on oval tiers.

Push floral bouquet spikes into bottom border of square tier: 1 large at each corner and 2 small centered at each side. Place remaining tulle puffs in flower spikes; push puff spikes and lengths of curled ribbon along bottom border to fill in any bare areas.

At reception: Assemble tiers on pillars. Position fondant covered cake boards, then swans; add small flower bouquets and ornament. Push spiked pillar floral bouquet into cake behind swans.

ADRIFT ON A DREAM

Lighter-than-air tulle draping creates a sophisticated impression, accented by lovely, easy-to-make ribbon roses. Serves 172.

ACCESSORIES YOU'LL NEED:

- 8, 10, 12, 14 in. Round Pans
- Tips 2, 5, 104
- Flower Nail No. 9
- 10, 12, 16 in. Tall Tier Stand Plates
- 6½ in. Columns (2 needed)
- 7¾ in. Column
- Top Column Cap Nut
- Bottom Column Bolt
- Glue-On Plate Legs
- 6mm Pearl Beading (2 pkgs. needed)*
- Dowel Rods
- Cake Dividing Set
- Cake Boards
- Meringue Powder
- Cake Corer Tube
- White Silk Leaves (2 pkgs. needed)
- 15 yds. White Tulle (6 inches wide)
- Royal, Buttercream Icings, p. 118
- Ornament: *Lustrous Love*

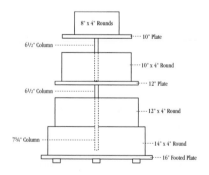

Using royal icing, tip 104 and Flower Nail No. 9, make 78 ribbon roses using royal icing, tip 104 and Flower Nail No. 7: Hold decorating bag at 90° angle with wide end of tip touching center of flower nail. Turn the nail counterclockwise, and using even pressure, squeeze out a ribbon of icing, wrapping it around to form a rose. Make extras to allow for breakage and let dry.

Prepare 2-layer cakes for center column construction (p. 112).

Divide 8 in. cake into 5ths, 10 in. into 6ths, 12 in. into 7ths and 14 in. into 8ths. Mark garlands 1¼ in. deep from top edge of cake. Drape pearls on cakes at garland marks.

For tulle draping: Cut a 20 in. x 6 in. length of tulle and fold in half, tie a knot at each end. Cover knots with royal icing; let dry. Push knotted ends of tulle into cakes ½ in. from top. Pipe tip 5 bead top border and double bead bottom border on all cakes (add bottom border for 8 in. cake at reception). Position pearl beading between double bead border. Attach leaves and roses. Pipe tip 2 dots on tulle.

For tulle in between tiers: Cut 7 lengths of tulle, each 36 inches long, 6 in. wide. Fold 36 inch lengths twice to form 9-inch pieces, then tie knot in center of each 9-inch length. Position 3 tulle pieces between 8 and 10 in. layers; 4 pieces between 10 and 12 in. layers.

Position ribbon rose and 3 leaves to cover knot.

At reception; Attach 2 - 6½ in. columns together and bolt to bottom column bolt. Add 12 in. plate with 7¾ in. column, then 10 in. plate and top column cap nut. Position 8 in. tier and pipe tip 5 double bead bottom border, add pearl beading between bead border. Position ornament.

*Remove pearls before cutting and serving.

ROSES ARISE

A graceful necklace of two-tone roses surrounds each heart-shaped tier, focusing the eye on your beautiful ornament. Serves 124.

ACCESSORIES YOU'LL NEED:

- Heart Pan Set (9, 12, 15 in. pans used)
- Tips 2, 2A, 3, 7, 10, 12, 352 (1 each needed); 102, 103, 104, 124, 125, 126 (2 each needed for two-tone roses)
- Flower Nail No. 7
- Rose, Willow Green Icing Colors
- Meringue Powder
- Cake Boards
- Fanci Foil Wrap
- Tuk-N-Ruffle

- Wooden Dowel Rods
- Royal, Buttercream Icings
- Ornament: *Our Dance*

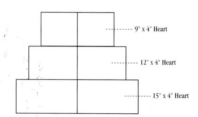

9" x 4" Heart
12" x 4" Heart
15" x 4" Heart

(Make roses in advance. Largest roses will take at least 48 hours to dry.)

Make two-tone roses in royal icing: 16 tip 126 with tip 2A bases; 12 tip 125 with tip 2A bases; 15 tip 124 with tip 2A bases; 20 tip 104 with tip 12 bases; 12 tip 103 with tip 10 bases; 20 tip 102 with tip 7 bases; and 30 tip 103 rosebuds. Let dry thoroughly.

When roses are completely dry, turn over and, in royal icing, pipe tip 12 pull-out spike on bottoms. Let dry. This will be used to position roses securely into cake.

Ice and prepare 2-layer cakes for stacked construction. Pipe tip 12 double bead bottom border on all cakes. Add tip 103 ruffle to bottom border of 15 in. cake.

With small angled spatula, gradually make descending lines from back to front of cakes to be used as a guide for positioning roses. Attach roses with dots of icing, pressing spikes into cake. Position rosebuds and add tip 3 sepals and calyxes; add tip 352 leaves. Add tip 2 dots on tops and sides of cakes above roses.

At reception, position ornament.

AUTUMN'S ILLUSION

Use your wedding cake to set a scene...and what setting could be more romantic than a quaint New England chapel at the peak of autumn color? Vibrant orange, red and yellow blossoms can be picked up in your draperies and table cloths. The chapel is easily made using patterns in this book and cookie dough. Serves 439.

ACCESSORIES YOU'LL NEED:

- 8 and 10 in. Round Pans
- 10*, 12 and 16 in. Square Pans
- Tips 3, 4, 18, 32, 47, 224, 233 and 352
- Ivory, Moss Green, Golden Yellow, Orange and Red-Red Icing Colors
- Crystal-Clear Cake Divider Set (1 each 10 and 12 in. plates used)
- 7 in. Crystal-Clear Twist Legs (2 pkgs. needed)
- Meringue Powder
- Decorator Brush Set
- Wooden Dowel Rods (1 pkg. needed)
- Small Doves (1 pkg. needed)
- Cake Dividing Set
- Church, Steeple Patterns, pgs. 122-123
- Fresh Flowers
- Royal, Buttercream Icings, p. 118
- Roll-Out Cookie Dough Recipe, p. 119
- Ornament: *Petite Happiest Day Couple*

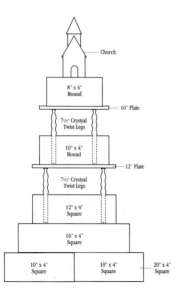

Using royal icing, make 390 (120 yellow†, 150 orange†, 120 red†) tip 224 drop flowers with tip 3 dot centers. (†To achieve shade shown, tint white royal icing ivory before adding specific flower colors.) Make extras to allow for breakage and let dry.

Use royal icing and smooth side of tip 47 to pipe "boards" for fence; make 18 at 2½ in., 28 at 2¼ in., 28 at 2 in. and 20 at 1¾ in.. Trim ends immediately to form point. Make extras to allow for breakage and let dry.

Cut Church and Steeple Patterns from cookie dough; bake and cool. Ice smooth with royal icing; let dry. Mark windows and doors with pencil. Assemble church and steeple with royal icing. Using decorator brush, paint stained glass windows with thinned down royal icing. Pipe tip 47 smooth side bands at corners of church. Pipe tip 3 string trim around doors and windows and for cross; add tips 3 and 4 beads at roof and steeple edges and trim on bands. Add tip 3 drop strings, ½ in. deep, on roof.

Paint doves with thinned down royal icing; let dry. Attach flowers to church. Pipe tip 352 leaves. Position birds.

Ice and prepare 2-layer cakes for stacked and pillar construction.
*The 20 in. square cake is assembled from four 2-layer 10 in. square cakes.

Mark all square cakes the same for drop strings: 3 in. wide and 1¾ in. deep. Divide 10 in. round cake into 10ths, mark center of each garland 1¾ in. deep.

Decorate all cakes except 8 in. round as follows: Pipe tip 3 triple drop strings. Pipe tip 32 shell bottom border and tip 18 reverse shell top border. Add drop flowers and tip 352 leaves.

On 8 in. round, pipe tip 233 grass around bottom of cake and plate. Attach flowers to cake, then attach fence pieces, descending from largest to smallest, then ascending. Attach flowers to top border and add tip 352 leaves.

At reception, assemble cake, add fence to 16 in. square cake and position church. Add fresh flowers and ornament.

THE
HOTEL
RECEPTION

The Formal Reception — Is it right for you?

Up to this point, we have taken a close-up look at

weddings that are, for the most part, "intimate" in terms

of the number of guests, and somewhat casual in overall

style. But if you're like many brides, your dream

wedding means nothing less than fancy and formal!

Therefore, we mustn't overlook the large, formal

wedding that many brides prefer and which many

weddings require. Although planning a formal recep-

tion takes much time and effort, the memories of a

once-in-a-lifetime "dream day" reward all your work.

At many hotels—even the finest—your choice of china, flatware and stemware can be limited. Although these three elements remain identitcal in each photo, our florist and event planner create a variety of exciting themes using fresh flowers and linen patterns.

Although brochures are helpful in giving you ideas in the beginning, never book your event without seeing your space in person. Stay organized as you look at hotels—you'll be surprised at how quickly your memories of each hotel blend together. Consult this list of details to note as you visit various locations. (Also, Polaroid snapshots can make wonderful reference photos.)

• Hotel name, address and phone
• Parking—is there adequate space for your guests? Is valet parking an option?
• Front entrance—Does the front entrance area seem inviting and well-maintained?
• Distinguishing interior preferences (marble floors, high ceilings, chandeliers, artwork, staircases, woodwork, etc.,)
• Overall colors and mood (bright, cheery, masculine, warm, cool, airy, etc.)
• Architectural style (antiques, modern, Victorian, etc.)
• Ballroom choices, sizes and styles. Vestibules for receiving/cocktail areas
• Will the room accommodate the number of guests plus music and dancing?
• Restroom accessibility
• View kitchen for cleanliness
• Elevators
• Backdrops for pictures
• Traffic flow
• Privacy—will other hotel guests or large groups be seen or heard during your reception?
• Did the hotel staff seem friendly and professional?
• Inquire about room accommodations and wedding night packages
• Ask for references of recent brides
• What did you like the most about this hotel? What did you like the least?

Keep these notes in a folder or binder along with accompanying snapshots.

This binder will be extremely helpful in narrowing down your list of options, especially if your fiancee cannot attend all the visits with you. Your next step will be to make appointments with the Director of Catering for each of the hotels you like best. This is when you can obtain more detailed information on menu ideas and costs.

THE ART OF NEGOTIATING

The task of choosing your hotel setting is both exciting and challenging. As you shop around, one of the most important things to remember is to get everything in writing and to make sure you understand each and every detail. This is perhaps the biggest—and most costly party you will ever throw, so make sure you do it right.

Let the hotel know that you are shopping around and that you're looking for the best deal and the best service. Depending on the city and location, you may find that the hotel industry can be quite competitive—why not make this work to your advantage?

There are many ways a hotel can go the extra mile to accommodate you if they really want your business. If not, don't be afraid to inquire about perks such as wedding night packages and hotel room accommodations for out of town guests, complimentary meals for guests, etc. You may also want to get a room or two for your bridal party as a pre-wedding meeting room. You should at least be able to get a discounted rate on a block of rooms, or a free/discounted bridal suite as part of your overall wedding package.

Also, when selecting your hotel, don't underestimate the importance of getting along with the staff. If, at this point, you don't feel you are being treated as an important client, then

chances are you will be treated this way throughout your entire planning period. Make sure you are dealing with someone who is excited about your event and who will do everything possible to make sure it happens the way YOU want it to.

THE CONTRACT

In order to properly evaluate your hotel options and your total wedding package, have the hotel(s) that you are seriously considering prepare a contract which outlines all services and associated costs. The following points should be outlined in any reception contract:

• Confirm reception date and times
• Confirm number of guests.
• Note the names of your preferred ballroom.
• Details of Cocktail and Hors d'oeuvres hour
• Style of dinner reception (buffet or served)
• Menu
• Music
• Staffing requirements
• Liquor/Corkage fees
• Gratuities
• Details of Wedding Night Package
• Parking information
• Overtime fees
• General restrictions
• Terms for payment
• Satisfaction Policies
• Miscellaneous Guarantees

Make sure these points are included and you understand all of them.

And remember, to avoid any surprises…

1) Don't forget to read the fine print—ASK QUESTIONS!

2) If it seems too good to be true—look for a catch.

3) Document any changes and the associated costs.

YOUR MENU

Choosing the meal for your guests requires thoughtful consideration and planning. Depending on your wedding theme and budget, the menu options presented to you will vary widely. The selection of your menu will be one of the most important planning decisions you will make, so keep your priorities in mind, be creative, and get the most out of your menu and your chef.

Mark Baker, executive chef at the Four Seasons Hotel in Chicago, has created a wedding menu for us that is both stunning and delicious. Although his selection of courses has been carefully orchestrated, he shares with us some "tricks of the trade" that make menu selection easy and affordable.

"Composing a special menu doesn't mean you have to select expensive items that have long, fancy names. The presentation of your meal can make a big difference in how your guests perceive it. Stay away from typical presentation techniques if you want to add interest to your meal," Baker suggests, "and don't forget to keep your guests in mind when selecting your menu," he adds.

Here are some other ways to get the most out of your wedding menu:

• Choose simple dishes. Don't over sauce or over spice and choose items that will appeal to a large crowd.
• Garnish but don't overcrowd your plate.
• "Compose" your plate—don't just choose a menu. Consider the color, shape, texture and flavor of your foods.
• Bright colored sauces or flavored oils add excitement to a simple piece of beef, chicken or fish.

• Try wrapping vegetables into "bundles" with lettuce leaves or chives for an interesting presentation.
• Hollowed out fruits and vegetables which are then filled can also add flair.
• Edible flowers turn any plate into a romantic meal.
• If your budget is tight, choose a less expensive entree, but do something unique with it. For instance, instead of beef tenderloin, you can substitute chicken. Stuff it with spinach or wrap it in phylo dough—or serve it with a rich, colorful sauce and a bright vegetable to make your plate more dramatic.
• Always ask your chef to prepare a trial meal for you. Together you can taste your options and come up with creative ideas that will make your wedding menu one to remember.

OUR HOTEL MENU

APPETIZER

Charcoal grilled portobello mushroom terrine with tomato, baby artichokes and salsify served with a trio of chive oil, red pepper oil and 100 year old balsamic vinegar. The plate is garnished with honmeishimiji mushrooms, chive and tomatoes.

SALAD

Radicchio cup filled with baby field greens, topped with edible pansies, then garnished with endive spears and a drizzle of arugula oil and balsamic vinegar.

ENTREE

Noisette of beef tenderloin with ragout of wild mushrooms. Served with spring asparagus, baby carrots and roasted potatoes with rosemary and thyme, and accented with a red wine sauce.

DESSERTS

Dessert station features a decadent assortment of gourmet cakes and tortes to be presented and served to each guest table.

FEATURE DESSERT

Layers of flourless chocolate cake and caramelized fresh bananas are nestled between almond wafers, chocolate, and topped with a chocolate "grid" and caramel rod. This tower sits atop a dramatic display of rich chocolate sauce.

WORKING WITH THE HOTEL STAFF

Once you have accomplished the challenge of choosing your hotel, it's time to focus on an even more tedious task—the reception details. As you begin this process, you will start builidng a relationship with the individual(s) on the hotel catering staff who will handle your event. Since these people will have ultimate responsiblity for executing the many components of your reception, it is critical that your interaction with them be honest, open and creative.

To get things off to a good start, an introductory meeting is recommended. In this initial meeting, you will most likely be introduced to the director of catering, who you should consider to be your primary contact person. At first, you will want to talk about general themes, including style, colors, flowers and overall tone of your wedding. You should be as explicit as possible since the director of catering will need to have a complete vision of your wedding in mind in order to do an effective job for you.

Over the course of your planning period, you will have dozens of meetings and conversations with your hotel catering director. It is important that you are free with your opinions and that you feel comforatable with the job he or she is doing. Remember, too, that it's her job to listen and to make things easier for you—that's what you pay her for. The better the catering director understands your desires, the happier you will be with the results.

It is most likely that your contact at the hotel has catered hundreds of events prior to yours . When she makes a suggestion that you don't like, don't be afraid to tell her so and to offer creative ideas of your own. She is trained to not take criticism personally. On the contrary, your honest feedback helps make her job easier and together you will find a workable solution. The old expression, "two heads are better than one" really rings true.

Unlike weddings at home where many of the details are handled spontaneously, every detail of a hotel reception should be carefully orchestrated. Although your hotel liaison will have the most responsibility for coordination, your involvement will still be quite significant. If you're a busy bride who wants to leave the planning details up to the professionals, then you might consider a wedding planner or consultant to be your "spokesperson" when dealing with the hotel staff. Whether you decide to manage your own details, or you hire someone else to manage them for you, just remember that communication is the key to a successful event.

CHOOSING YOUR MENU

Your menu will be one of your primary planning concerns. Here are a few factors that will help guide you. Consider the season and time of day. A late morning or mid-day wedding may call for a brunch or luncheon menu, while a late afternoon or evening wedding will require a heavier dinner menu. The director of catering should present a number of options and suggestions for you. And don't forget about your budget! The options presented to you should not exceed the costs you have allotted per guest. It's a good idea to know up front what you are able to spend per guest and still stay within your budget.

Determine the formality of your wedding reception. Your menu should be consistent with the formal tone you are setting. Keep in mind that hotel weddings are seldom casual. Most hotel weddings are considered formal, with women in dresses and men in suits. However if you really want to go all out, you may want to state "black tie" or "black tie optional" on your invitations, in which case the men will wear tuxedos and women will wear more formal evening wear. If you do decide to have a very formal reception, then be sure to carry that tone throughout all of your reception details—including your menu.

COCKTAILS AND HORS D'OEUVRES

There are a number of ways to offer a cocktail hour if you choose to have one. Many couples prefer to have an open bar for their guests as soon as they arrive, while others prefer to delay the open bar until after dinner. If you don't want to go the expense of having an open bar both before and after dinner, a nice alternative might be to serve chilled champagne during cocktails. You might also serve wine at your guests' tables during the meal, and then have an open bar after dinner when your entertainment begins. Other options include champagne punch, beer and wine only, or a special dessert station that would serve after dinner drinks such as brandies and cognacs. You may also have champagnes and wines passed on trays by servers, or you can have guests help themselves at a cocktail station. When it comes to liquor, make sure you are comfortable with what you are serving your guests and once again, remember the budget.

Hors d'oeuvres also offer many serving options. You might want guests to help themselves at a buffet, or you may consider having servers pass your hors d'oeuvres. Regardless, make sure the items you choose are easy to eat in a bite or two. If you do decide to have your hors d'oeuvres passed, make sure you have plenty to distribute evenly throughout your room. Sometimes the guests at far corners of the room have a harder time getting to the hors d'oeuvres, while guests just outside the kitchen have plenty.

With the help of your director of catering, choose a nice variety of hors d'oeuvres for your guests, and don't overdo it. Today, people are eating healthier and lighter, so it isn't necessary to have an excessive hors d'oeuvres table featuring many heavy foods. Use discretion in serving seafood, such as shrimp, crab, or lobster—particularly if you need to watch your budget. If serving chilled shrimp to all your guests is a little too steep for you, ask your director of catering if there is an item featuring shrimp as an ingredient instead. This will stretch the budget and still provide a lovely, high-class hors d'oeuvres assortment for your guests.

DINNER AND DESSERT OPTIONS

Your dinner menu will take the biggest bite out of your budget, so plan carefully. There are two main dinner styles to choose from at hotel receptions—buffet and served. Be sure to discuss the price differences for both options with your director of catering. Either option can be presented beautifully and there are many creative menu choices available. One popular method of serving a buffet style meal is by having multiple food stations for your guests. For instance, you might have a pasta bar where your guests choose their own pasta, ingredients and sauces—or a stir-fry station with a chef preparing Oriental favorites made-to-order. These are fun, delicious and a little less traditional than many standard wedding fares. And finally, be sure to inquire about homestyle or family style meals—a very traditional style for many ethnic cultures where platters of foods are served at each table and shared by guests.

Your variety of dessert options is as wide as your dinner choices. Of course, the "star" dessert should be your wedding cake. However there are other options to consider. Sweet tables are extremely popular as an accompaniment to cake, coffee and after dinner drinks. Petit fours, pastries, chocolates, nuts and cookies make a lovely buffet to accent your cake. Ice cream can also be served along with the wedding cake, or the cake can be sliced and wrapped for your guests to take home. Don't be afraid to get creative. If your budget can handle it, why not have a gourmet crepe station or even a hot fudge sundae station for your guests to indulge themselves in? This is also an opportunity for chocolate-lovers to go crazy. So have fun, and remember dessert is the last thing your guests will experience at your wedding, so be sure to leave them with a decadent impression that's sure to last!

ENTERTAINMENT AND OTHER WEDDING SERVICES

Your director of catering can advise you on every aspect of your reception and has referrals for every imaginable wedding service provider. Although the beauty of a hotel reception is having everything handled under one roof, there may be some other wedding services for which you may have your own preferences. Below is a list of outside services to remember. If you do not have preferences of your own, your director of catering can bring them in for you:
• Florist—he or she should be consulted early on in your planning to help create overall themes and color schemes.
•Transportation—to and from the ceremony, to the hotel, to the airport.
• Linen Rentals—the hotel will have standard linens, however, if you have special requirements, you may have to obtain them independently.

• Music—Instrumentalists during cocktails, DJ. or orchestra
• Video Production & Photographer—make arrangements for them to visit the space prior to the event.
• Make-up professional—for bride and bridal party. Some hotels may have salon professionals on staff.

TIPPING

Tipping can be a very awkward subject, since nothing is really written in stone and specific expectations are rarely communicated. However it might help to know the people who are behind the scenes making your reception all come together in case you do decide to tip them:
• Director of Catering—your liaison with the hotel.
• Banquet Manager—heads up kitchen staff and executes entire event.
• Captains—the head waiters on the floor.

LIQUOR PACKAGES AND GRATUITIES

Of all the components of your wedding package, your liquor arrangements should be the most carefully reviewed. Also, be aware of the restrictions that many hotels have in regard to liquor. Here are some valuable tips when creating your liquor contract:
• Prices listed may include ++ (plus, plus). This refers to tax and tip which are added to the listed price. To be on the safe side, figure 10% tax and 17% tip additional.
• Do not expect to bring in your own liquor. If by rare chance you are permitted to do so, expect to pay a corkage fee for chilling and serving.
• Always buy liquor by consumption or "by the glass" — not by the hour.
• Figure on 2.5 drinks per person at a typical open bar setting before dinner. Assume the same for after dinner.
• CHECK ALL BILLS AGAINST YOUR CONTRACT!

DREAM CASTLE

A real-life storybook ending for your wedding day. This majestic castle is an attraction all its own...intricate stringwork and stately pearl beading, together with crown and ruffle border treatments, forge a dramatic ascent to the summit. Its grand scale makes this the ideal cake for the larger reception. Serves 668.

ACCESSORIES YOU'LL NEED:

- 10, 14 in. Round Pans
- 18 in. Half Round Pan
- Tips 1, 2, 3, 4, 14, 18, 21, 199, ID, 2B, 4B, 127D
- Meringue Powder
- Small, Large Hexagon Castle Base Patterns; Small and Large Windows, Door Patterns (see pgs. 126-127)
- Plastic Dowel Rods (2 pkgs. needed for castle)
- Dowel Rods
- 4mm and 6mm Pearl Beading* (5 pkgs., 4mm, 6 pkgs., 6mm needed)
- Cake Boards, Fanci-Foil Wrap
- Cake Dividing Set
- 7½ in. and 9 in. Crystal-Clear Twist Pillars (1 pkg. each needed)
- Crystal-Clear Cake Divider Set Plates, 10 in., 12 in., 16 in. (1 each)
- 4 in. Lollipop Sticks
- Waxed paper
- Hot glue gun
- Styrofoam (craft blocks)
- One 20 in. and four 18 in. round sturdy corrugated cardboard or plywood bases
- Fresh flowers and greenery
- Buttercream, Royal Icings, p. 118
- Sugar Cones
- Ornament: *Our Day Couple*

*Remove pearl beading before cutting and serving.

Construct castle components using royal icing. Using hexagon patterns and 3½ in. circle, cut styrofoam with serrated edge knife or band saw as follows: Large Hexagon 6 in. high; Small Hexagon 3 in. high; Round 3 in. high. Ice styrofoam tops and sides smooth, let dry, add a second coat if necessary. Let dry completely. Make 11 turrets as follows: **Peaks**—using sugar cones and tip 127D, cover a 2½ in. deep area from tip, allow icing to set 3-5 minutes, then smooth with spatula or pat smooth with hand dusted with cornstarch. Let dry 24 hours. **Columns**—Cut plastic dowel rods into lengths indicated below using scissors or sharp craft knife; some columns will need half of the bottom trimmed off to allow positioning flush on castle corners—measure length indicated up from bottom of column, cut a slit up through dowel rod at the half way point and cut side off. For Large Hexagon tier cut six 3 in. columns with 2 in. trimmed; for Small Hexagon cut one 6 in. column with 3 in. trimmed and one 3½ in. column with 2 in. trimmed; for Round cut one 4 in. column with 2 in. trimmed, one 3 in. column with 1½ in. trimmed and one 3¼ in. column (no trim). **Decorate columns:** Pipe tip ID smooth side band at top edge, overpipe with tip 2B band. Let dry 24 hours. Attach peaks to columns using tip 2. Cover with tip 2 cornelli lace. Divide bands around columns into 5ths and pipe tip 2 drop strings. Add 6mm pearl beading at top of bands, 4mm pearl beading at bottom. Position tur-

rets on lollipop sticks inserted in craft block to dry. Ice 10 in. plate smooth in royal icing, let dry.

Assemble and decorate castle: Use hot glue to attach components and assemble; decorating is done in royal icing. Stack tiers on 10 in. plate as follows: Offset top round tier ½ in. to back; middle hexagon tier is centered; bottom large hexagon is offset to back of plate to accommodate ornament. Begin decorating at the top tier and work down; refer to construction directions above for turret sizes appropriate to each tier. **Top Tier:** Attach top and side turrets. For top border, pipe tip ID smooth side band; overpipe with tip 2B smooth side band; attach 4mm beading to bottom edge of band. Divide top edge of band into approx. 1 in. segments; pipe tip 2 double drop strings between division marks. Mark Small Window patterns ¼ in. up from bottom edge. Cover window areas with tip 2 lattice; trim with 4mm pearl beading. Pipe tip 199 band around base of center turret and at bottom border of tier; trim with 4mm pearl beading. Add tip 199 fleur-de-lis at base of side turrets; trim columns with tip 4 beads. Pipe tip 4 double row of beads on tier top, add 6mm pearl beading. **Middle Tier:** Attach turrets, and pipe top border as above. Pipe tip ID smooth side band at bottom border, overpipe with tip 2B smooth side. Add tip 199 stripe. Position 4mm pearl beading. Mark window ¾ in. high x 1½ in. wide on each side. Cover window area with tip

2 lattice and trim with 4mm pearl beading. Pipe tip 4 double row of beads on tier top, add 6mm pearl beading. Pipe tip 4 triple bead border at corners. **Bottom Tier:** Mark Door Pattern, aligning at bottom edge of cake. Mark Large Window Patterns 1 ½ in. from top and bottom, centering on each side. Attach turrets to corners; pipe top border as above. Cover window area with tip 2 lattice, trim with 4mm pearl beading; trim door with 6mm pearl beading. Pipe tip 1D smooth side band and tip 199 line for bottom border; trim with 4mm and 6mm pearl beading. Pipe tip 199 fleur-de-lis on columns; trim column with tip 4 triple beads. Pipe tip 4 double row of beads on tier top, add 6mm pearl beading. Pipe tip 4 triple bead border at corners.

Ice 2-layer cakes smooth and prepare for push-in pillar and stacked construction. For 18 in. round tier, bake four 18 in. half rounds each 2 in. high. **Note:** When assembling the four stacked 10 in. and 14 in. cakes that make up the bottom platform, offset the 10 in. tiers to align within approx. ½ inch of the 14 in. tiers edge. Dowel rod those four cakes on areas where tiered cake will be positioned; also dowel rod 10 in. top tier for placement of castle.

10 in. Tier: Using Cake Dividing Set, divide cake into 8ths. Pipe tip 1D smooth side band around bottom border; cover with tip 2 lattice; trim with 6mm pearl beading. Pipe tip 18 zigzag garland approximately 2 in. deep between division marks; pipe tip 3 double drop strings above garland. Pipe tip 3 vertical lines approximately 1 in. long on garland; trim with tip 3 dots. Add 4 mm pearl beading. Pipe tip 18 top shell border. Pipe tip 199 upright shells at division marks; trim with tip 3 dots.

14 in. Tier: Divide cake into 16ths. Using tip 3, pipe drop strings between division marks, alternating sections of 2 strings and 4 strings. First string is dropped 1 in. deep, each additional string is dropped ¼ in. below. Add 4mm pearl beading for final string. Pipe tip 18 top shell border. Add tip 199 upright shell and tip 3 dot at division marks. Pipe tip 4B bottom shell border. Add tip 14 diagonal zigzag to each shell, then pipe tip 14 zigzag to edge plate. Add 6mm pearl beading. (Tip 14 zigzag on plate and pearl beading can be added at reception.)

18 in. Tier: Divide cake into 16ths. Pipe tip 2 drop strings 2 in. deep between division marks, cover area with tip 2 lattice. Pipe tip 18 zigzag garland, add 4mm pearl beading. Pipe tip 3 drop string ½ in. below garland; pipe three drop strings from each, add tip 3 dots. Pipe tip 21 top shell border. Add tip 199 upright shell at points, add tip 3 dots. Pipe tip 4B bottom shell border. Add tip 14 diagonal zigzag on top. Pipe tip 14 zigzag around plate edge, add 6mm pearl beading. (Tip 14 zigzag

on plate and pearl beading can be added at reception.)

10 and 14 in. Stacked Tiers **10 in.:** Decorate as 10 in. tier above. Hint: Add tip 18 top shell border at reception after cake has been assembled; or if decorated prior to reception, do not pipe shells on 3 divisions where tiered cake will be positioned.

14 in.: Divide cake into 12ths (mark at top and 2 in. up from bottom). Bottom border: Build a base for ruffle to rest on—pipe tip 199 stripe around bottom border; pipe tip 2B smooth side band angled over stripe. On this base, pipe tip 127D ruffle, alternating straight sections with ruffle sections. Cover straight swag sections with tip 3 lines; pipe tip 18 zigzag garland on top edge; pipe three tip 3 double drop strings from garland ½ and 1 in. deep. On ruffle section, pipe tip 18 zigzag garland. Attach 6mm pearl beading to garland, add tip 18 rosettes. Pipe tip 3 beads at ruffle edge. Pipe top crown border—within each division mark pipe six tip 199 upright shells; pipe tip 3 double drop strings between the second and fifth shells of each section. Add tip 3 dots.

Ornament: Using royal icing, pipe tip 1 e-motion crown on bride.

At reception: Position four stacked tiers and assemble tiers on pillars. Position castle on top tier. Add ornament. Arrange flowers and greenery. Position 6mm pearls around base of 14 in. bottom tiers.

Note: For support, 18 in. tier should be on plywood base. For center support under main cake, put a foil-covered wood block or styrofoam block the height of 10 and 14 in. stacked cakes with boards under 18 in. tier when assembling.

COVENTRY ARCHES

A breathtaking example of the Lambeth style: overpiped scrolls, loops and lattice teardrops create a spectacular dimensional impact. Because many of these bands link the tiers, be sure to follow our top-to-bottom instructions. Serves 220.

ACCESSORIES YOU'LL NEED:

- 7, 9 (2 Pan Set), 10, 14, 16 in. Round Pans
- Tips ID, 2, 2A, 2B, 3, 5, 7, 14, 32, 48, 224, 225, 349, 362, 363, 364, 789
- Violet Icing Color
- Teardrop Pattern, p. 134
- 5 in. Grecian Spiked Pillars (1 pkg. needed)
- Dowel Rods
- 8 in. Separator Plate (1 needed)
- Decorator Favorites Pattern Press Set (Small and large scroll used)
- Meringue Powder
- Cake Board, Fanci-Foil Wrap
- 9-Pc. Flower Former Set
- Cake Dividing Set
- Buttercream, Royal Icings, p. 118
- Ornament: *Forevermore*

Using royal icing, make 200 tip 224 drop flowers and 400 tip 225 drop flowers; both with tip 2 dot centers. Make extras to allow for breakage. Let dry.

Several days before reception (up to 2 weeks), make the following royal icing bands: On large flower formers, make 16 tip 789 smooth side bands; on medium flower formers, make 28 tip 2B serrated bands; 16 tip ID serrated bands and 12 tip 48 serrated bands. **To make bands:** Cover back of flower formers with waxed paper. Pipe across backs of formers.

Attach tip ID bands to top of tip 789 bands with royal icing. Pipe tip 2 lattice on tip ID band. Using small scroll pattern press, trace horizontal scroll on top and bottom of tip 789 band. For scrolls on top, bottom and sides of band, pipe tip 14 outline, then overpipe with tips 5, 3 and then 2. Pipe tip 3 beads along sides of tip 789 band and around lattice; add tip 3 dots. Let dry. Position drop flowers in center of lattice and add tip 349 leaves. Let dry.

For large teardrops (16 needed): Trace pattern on paper and cover with waxed paper. With royal icing, pipe tip 2A shell and let dry slightly. Pipe tip 2 lattice over shell. Let dry.

For small (24 needed) and large (44 needed) scrolls: Using small and large scroll pattern presses, trace on cardboard, cover with waxed paper. **Large scroll:** In royal icing, pipe tip 362 royal icing outline, overpipe with tips 7, 5, 3 and 2. Let dry. **Small scroll:** Pipe tip 362 outline, overpipe with tips 5, 3 and 2. Let dry. Ice and prepare 1-layer 9 in. cake and 16 in. cake, 2-layer 7 in. and 10 in. cake, and 3-layer 14 in. cake, for stacked and push-in pillar construction.

2-layer 7 in. cake: Divide into 12ths. Mark ¾ in. up from bottom for scrolls. On top edge of tier, mark 1 in. down and 1 in. apart for crown border. Pipe tip 363 shell bottom border. Place small royal icing scrolls at marks on cake sides. Attach with dots of icing. Position drop flowers and tip 349 leaves. On top border, pipe tip 32 crown border and tip 3 double drop strings. Position drop flowers.

1-layer 9 in. cake: Divide in 12ths. At center of divisions, mark 1 in. down from top for drop strings. Position large royal icing scrolls on top edge between division marks. Pipe tip 3 drop strings, 1 in. deep.

2-layer 10 in. cake: Divide in 12ths. At center of each division, mark 1½ in. down from top for drop strings. At 12ths division mark, measure 2¼ in. down from top for placement of scroll. Pipe tip 364 shell bottom border. Position drop flowers in a crescent shape over shells; add tip 349 leaves. Position tip 2B royal icing bands on top edge of cake. Position small royal icing scrolls on side at 2¼ in. mark. Pipe tip 3 drop strings, 1½ in. deep. Position tip 48 bands, attaching from top of 9 in. tier to top edge of 10 in. tier. Add drop flowers on and behind bands; add tip 349 leaves. Under side scrolls, pipe tip 2 bead scallops. Pipe tip 3 double drop strings on edge of bands, single drop strings on bottom edge of scroll. Add tip 2 dots.

3-layer 14 in. cake: Divide in 16ths. Mark from bottom at division point, 1 in. for scrolls and 3½ in. for lowest point of bead arch. At center of 16ths division, mark 2½ in. up for teardrops. Pipe tip 362 shell bottom border. Attach teardrops with icing. Pipe tip 2 beads at edge of teardrops. Pipe tip 2 bead arch around teardrops; attach drop flower at point. Pipe tip 2 double drop strings from edge of scrolls, add tip 2 dots.

1-layer 16 in. cake: Divide in 16ths. Pipe tip 362 shell bottom border. Position tip 2B bands at division marks; position flowers, tip 349 leaves. Add tip 2 dots. Position tip 789 bands between tip 2B bands, attaching at base of 14 in. tier and board. Attach large scrolls at side of 14 in. tier. At reception, position tiers on pillars and ornament.

VICTORIAN CHARM

Recalling the romance of an era gone by: opulent sotas, soft rose hues and lavish ruffles.
This elaborate setting, highlighted by a magnificent floral fountain, is the perfect backdrop for
reception festivities. See page 114 for foolproof ways to set up your staircases. Serves 224.

ACCESSORIES YOU'LL NEED:

- 6, 10 in. Square Pans
- 12, 16 in. Round Pans
- Petite Heart Pan
- Tips 1, 3, 4, 6, 16, 18, 21, 101, 102, 124, 352
- Ivory*, Rose Petal Pink*, Willow Green Icing Colors
- Flower Nail No. 9
- Cake Boards, Fanci-Foil Wrap
- 14 in. Ruffle Board (1 needed)
- Dowel Rods
- Meringue Powder
- 6-Pc. Heart Cookie Cutter Set (1¾ in. wide cutter used)
- Cake Dividing Set
- Crystal-Look Bowl (1 needed)
- Crystal-Look Base (1 needed)
- Kolor Flo Fountain
- Flower Holder Ring
- 14 Pc. Arched Tier Set
- 3 in. and 5 in. Grecian Pillars (1 set each needed)
- 7 in. and 11 in. Square Separator Plates (2 each needed)
- Filigree Stairway (2 needed)
- Bridesmaids, Pearlized Blush (6 needed)
- Buttercream, Royal, Egg White, Royal Icings, p. 118
- Ornament: *I Do*

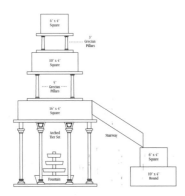

*Tint icing Ivory, add Rose Petal Pink to achieve Victorian Peach shade.

Using Egg White Royal Icing and Petite Heart Pan, make 20 filigree lace hearts: Generously grease the back side of Petite Heart Pan with shortening. Using Royal Egg White Recipe on p. 118, pipe tip 1 sotas on back of Petite Heart Pan, leaving bottom ¼ in edge free. When top is completely covered, pipe tip 1 bead border around bottom edge. Let dry on pan overnight. To remove from pan, hold inside of pan over low gas flame or electric burner to melt shortening. Gently remove lace hearts and place on waxed paper to completely dry overnight. Make extras to allow for breakage and let dry.

Using royal icing, make 32 tip 102 victorian roses with tip 6 bases; 92 tip 101 victorian roses with tip 4 bases; 60 tip 102 rosebuds; 60 tip 101 rosebuds. When forming a victorian rose, wrap petals around rather than moving up and down; pipe more petals than usual so that roses look partially opened; and pinch ends of petals with finger dipped in cornstarch. Make extras to allow for breakage and let dry.

Ice 2-layer tiers smooth and prepare for pillar and stacked construction.

For 12 in. and 16 in. round cakes: Using cake dividing set, divide 12 in. round into 8ths and 16 in. round into 12ths. Mark cake sides 2 in. up from bottom at division marks; pipe tip 18 shell bottom border, then tip 124 ruffle garland. Add tip 16 zigzag garland. Pipe tip 16 rosettes at garland points. Imprint heart cookie cutter between garland points. Using tip 3, outline and fill in hearts, smooth with finger dipped in cornstarch. Attach filigree lace hearts with dots of icing; edge with tip 3 beads. Cover 16 in. cake top with tip 1 sotas. Pipe tip 16 shells around separator plate. On top edge of cakes, position three small roses centered at division marks, curving downward toward hearts; add rosebuds to connect to hearts. Position large roses at bottom border. Add tip 352 leaves.

For 6 in. and 10 in. cakes: Divide 6 in. cake tops in half. Divide 10 in. cake top in thirds. Mark 1¾ in. deep from top edge of cakes for triangle shapes. Using tip 3, outline and pipe in triangles; smooth with finger dipped in cornstarch. Cover area with tip 1 sotas; edge with tip 3 beads. Pipe tip 1 drop strings and dots on triangle edges. Add tip 16 top shell borders and tip 18 bottom shell borders. Position roses and rosebuds, add tip 352 leaves.

At reception, arrange fresh flowers in Flower Holder Ring, Crystal Bowl and Crystal Base**. Assemble Kolor Flo Fountain and position with Flower Holder Ring; position tiers on pillars. Arrange stairways and position ornament and bridesmaids.

**Separate the Crystal Base into 2 sections and use the smaller as the floral container.

OUR SONG

Lovebirds singing and cherubs harmonizing set a lilting mood of romance. Dainty gum paste flowers and lattice work provide elegant accompaniment. Serves 190.

ACCESSORIES YOU'LL NEED:

- 4-Pc. Petal Pan Set (9 and 15 in. used)
- 16 in. Square Pan
- Tips I, 2, 2A, 5, 16, 18, 44, 127D, 349
- Creamy Peach, Golden Yellow, Moss Green Icing Colors
- Cake Board, Fanci-Foil Wrap
- Tuk-N-Ruffle
- Kneeling Cherub Fountain
- Musical Trio (2 sets needed)
- Flower Formers
- Gum Paste Mix
- 30-Pc. Gum Paste Flowers Kit (Baby's Breath and Apple Blossom Cutters Used)
- 10 in. Separator Plates (2 needed)
- 6 ½ in. Arched Pillars (I set needed)
- Buttercream Icing, p. 118
- Ornament: *Spring Song*

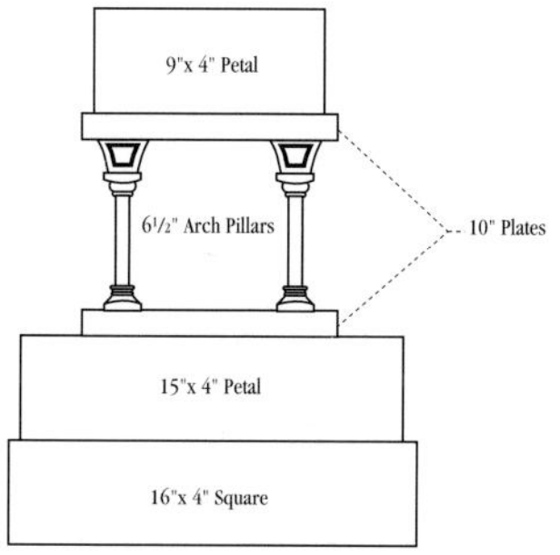

Prepare Gum Paste Mix; make 120 apple blossoms and 220 smaller blossoms using baby's breath cutter and following apple blossom instructions in Gum Paste Flowers Book. Position on flower formers. With royal icing, pipe tip I single and multi dot centers. Let set.

Ice and prpare cakes for stacked and pillar construction, p. 113.

For 9 in. Petal Cake: With toothpick, mark each petal division for garland 1½ inches down from top edge. Ice garland area smooth in peach. Pipe tip 2 lattice over garland area, add tip 16 zigzag garland. Pipe tip 16 top and tip 18 bottom shell borders.

For 15 in. Petal Cake: Ice alternating petals in peach. Mark remaining petals for garland, 1½ inches down from top edge. Ice garland areas smooth in peach. Pipe tip 44 lattice on solid peach petals and pipe tip 2 lattice on garland areas. Pipe tip 16 zigzag scallops at edge of garland; add tip 5 vertical beads between petal divisions. Pipe tip 16 top and tip 18 bottom shell borders. Edge bottom plate with tip 16 scallops.

For 16 in. Square Cake: Mark 1½ inches up from base. Pipe tip 2A line at base around entire cake, then pipe tip 127D ruffle. Pipe tip 44 lattice work above ruffle. Pipe tip 18 top shell border.

Using buttercream icing, position flowers on all cakes and add tip 349 leaves. Add flowers to ornaments.

At reception: Assemble cake, position ornament. Add a few flowers around musical trio's feet and in the kneeling cherub fountain.

9"x 4" Petal

6½" Arch Pillars — 10" Plates

15"x 4" Petal

16"x 4" Square

CELESTIAL VISION

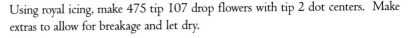

*A sparkling fountain flows serenely above an impressive foundation of tiers.
There's so much to delight the eye...leaf-framed angels, delicate bouquets, graceful bead garlands
and more. A wonderful design for champagne brunch or glamorous evening receptions.
Serves 319, saving one 6 in. cake for first anniversary.*

ACCESSORIES YOU'LL NEED:

- 6, 8 in. Round Pans
- 18 in. Half Round Pan
- Tips 2, 3, 4B, 16, 18, 19, 21, 101, 107, 349
- Decorator Favorites Pattern Press Set
- Cake Dividing Set
- 3 in. Grecian Pillars (6 pkgs. needed)
- 5 in. Grecian Pillars (1 pkg, needed)
- Hidden Pillars (2 pkgs. needed)
- Decorator Preferred Plates (Twelve 9 in., Two 12 in., One 18 in. needed)
- Plastic Dowel Rods
- Angel Duet (3 pkgs. needed)
- Musical Trio (2 pkgs. needed)
- Ring Bearer, Flower Girl
- Designer Bridesmaids, Dark Pink (3 pkgs. needed)
- Designer Groomsmen, Black Tux (3 pkgs. needed)
- Kolor-Flo Fountain
- Flower Holder Ring
- Meringue Powder
- Cake Boards, Fanci-Foil Wrap
- Crystal-Look Base (7 needed)
- 19 in. round triple thick corrugated cardboard or plywood base
- Wood or styrofoam blocks
- Fresh flowers, florist foam, white tulle
- Ornament: *Love's Duet*

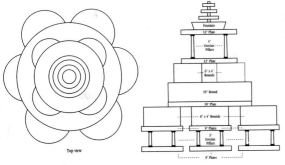

Top view

Using royal icing, make 475 tip 107 drop flowers with tip 2 dot centers. Make extras to allow for breakage and let dry.

Ice and prepare cakes for pillar and stacked construction. 6 in. and 8 in. cakes are 2 layers. Four 18 in. half rounds, 2 in. each, are stacked in two layers on 19 in. round foil-covered board. All tiers will need additional dowel rod support for positioning of cakes and fountain.

6 in. Tiers: Divide into 6ths at top edge; centered between each division, mark cake on side 1¾ in. down from top edge. Imprint small horizontal "c" pattern press above mark. Pipe tip 4B elongated shell, 1½ in. long, at top division marks. Using tip 16, add reverse shells to form fleur-de-lis, outline imprint. Using tip 3, pipe double drop strings between side division marks; overpipe with bead border; add dots at bottom of fleur-de-lis. Pipe tip 21 bottom and tip 18 top shell borders (pipe top border only on front half of each cake—plate will be resting on back half). Position flowers on top of elongated shell and add tip 349 leaves.

18 in. Tier: Divide into 6ths. Using 3" circle, trace circles on cake side at each division mark. Imprint vine pattern press between circles, reversing pattern to match design on each side. Pipe tip 101 sweet pea border around circle. Using tip 16, outline vine imprint with "c" scrolls; position flowers and add tip 349 leaves. Pipe tip 21 bottom and tip 19 top shell borders. Attach angels to circles with dots of icing.

8 in. Tiers: Divide into 8ths; mark 2 in. down on cake sides at every other division mark. Imprint vine pattern press at division marks ½ in. down from top edge of cake. At 2 in. mark, pipe tip 4B elongated shell, add tip 3 dot at bottom of shell; imprint small "c" scroll angled to the left and right 1 in. from bottom edge; outline imprints using tip 16. Using tip 3, pipe double drop string, overpipe with beads. Attach flowers and add tip 349 leaves. Pipe tip 21 bottom shell border. Add tip 18 top shell border at reception after assembly.

At reception, arrange fresh flowers in Crystal-Look Bases and flower ring. Assemble 8 in. bottom tiers, arranged in a circle, on 3 in. pillars and 9 in. plates. Use 18 in. plate to center cakes; mark position of hidden pillars on 8 in. cakes by imprinting feet of plate. Trim hidden pillars to cake height. Place wood or styrofoam block (measuring as tall as 6 in. cake and pillars) in center of cake group. Position 18 in. plate; add 18 in. tier and pipe tip 18 "c" motion to cover edge of foil-covered board. Assemble remaining tiers, pillars, flower ring, Musical Trio and fountain. Pipe tip 18 top shell border on 8 in. tiers. Position ornament.

HONEYMOON FLIGHT

Make your guests smile with this delightful bridal balloon. Dried beans, inserted before inflation, help shape and steady the balloon, which is then taped to dowel rods. Serves 181.

ACCESSORIES YOU'LL NEED:

- 6 in. (3 in. high) Round Pan
- 8, 12, 16 in. Round Pans
- Tips 2, 7, 14, 16, 18, 21, 31, 104, 125, 126, 127D, 193, 352
- Creamy Peach, Lemon Yellow, Leaf Green Icing Colors
- Star Patterns, p. 109
- Cake Dividing Set
- Cake Boards, Fanci-Foil Wrap
- 9 and 7 in. Crystal-look Spiked Pillars (1 set each needed)
- 7 and 14 in. Decorator Preferred Separator Plates (1 each needed)
- Dowel Rods
- Stamens, Yellow (7 pkgs. needed)
- Bomboniere!® 3/16 in. Instant Bow Ribbon, White (2 8yd. spools needed)
- Balloons, White
- Floral Puff Accent
- Meringue Powder
- Color Flow Mix
- Reluctant Groom Ornament
- Buttercream, Royal Icings, p. 118
- Waxed Paper, White Dry Beans
- Curling Ribbon

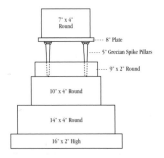

- Using Color Flow Mix, make 16 Color Flow stars (p. 119): Outline patterns using tip 2, then flow in centers. Make extras to allow for breakage and let dry.

- Make 350 drop flowers using royal icing: 175 yellow using tip 31 and 175 peach using tip 193. Add tip 14 green star centers and place 3 stamens in each.* Make extras to allow for breakage and let dry.

- Ice 1-layer 6 in. round and 2-layer 8, 12 and 16 in. round tiers smooth and prepare for push-in pillar and stacked construction.

- **6 in. tier:** Cover sides with tip 7 basketweave. Pipe tip 104 ribbon swag at bottom border. Position flowers and add tip 352 leaves on top border and cascading down sides.

- **8 in. tier:** Divide cake into 8ths. Pipe tip 125 ruffled garland 1¼ in. deep between division marks. Add tip 16 e-motion above garland. Pipe tip 18 c-scroll shell top border. Add tip 21 bottom shell border; position flowers and add tip 352 leaves. Attach stars at garland points using dots of icing.

- **12 in. tier:** Divide cake into 8ths, marking cake side 2 in. from top edge. Pipe tip 21 bottom shell border, then pipe tip 125 ruffled garland between division marks. Add tip 16 e-motion above garland. Pipe tip 18 c-scroll shell top border. Arrange flowers at division points, add tip 352 leaves. Attach stars at garland points using dots of icing.

- **16 in. tier:** Divide cake into 10ths, marking cake side 2 in. from top edge. Pipe tip 21 bottom shell border. Add tip 127D ruffled border, pipe tip 126 ruffled garland between division marks. Add tip 16 e-motion above garland. Pipe tip 21 c-scroll shell top border. Attach clusters of drop flowers centered between division marks at top border. Add tip 352 leaves. Attach stars at garland points using dots of icing.

- For balloon "strings": Cut four dowel rods into 10½ in. lengths. Remove the string from one package of Instant Bow Ribbon, save string and cover dowel rods with ribbon; glue in place. Make 4 instant bows following package directions, using 48 in. of ribbon for each; glue a bow to end of each rod. Set aside.

- At reception: Assemble tiers on pillars. Position Floral Puff Accent. Place approximately 2 tablespoons dry white beans in balloon and inflate. Push ends of ribbon-covered dowel rods in cake top, position ornament, position balloon on dowel rods and tape in place to secure. Place curling ribbon and string from Instant Bow Ribbon on balloon, securing with double-stick tape.

*Remove drop flowers before serving.

HEART ENCHANTMENT

A marriage of marvelous textures defines this exquisite cake.
Ruffles gently drape over a fringe-look band border, while a stately crested shell border
crowns each tier. An ideal choice for the smaller-scale reception. Serves 76.

ACCESSORIES YOU'LL NEED:

- 9, 15 in. Heart Pans
- Tips 2, 2A, 3, 16, 18, 89, 104, 225, 789
- Decorator Favorites Pattern Press (small "C" scroll press used)
- 16 in. Featherweight Decorating Bag
- Cake Boards, Fanci-Foil Wrap
- Meringue Powder
- 11 in. Heart Separator Plates (2 needed)
- 3 in. Grecian Pillars (1 set needed)
- 4mm Pearl Beading (1 pkg. needed)
- Crystal-look Bowl
- Buttercream, Royal Icings, p. 118
- Greenery
- Ornament: *Ribbon Delight*

Using royal icing and tip 225 make 80 drop flowers with tip 2 dot centers. Make extras to allow for breakage and let dry.

Prepare 2-layer cakes for pillar construction.

For 15 in. cake: Mark for band 1½ in. from bottom edge. Pipe a tip 2A line of icing at base of cake to support band. Using 16 in. decorating bag fitted with tip 789, pipe a slightly angled band below mark. Pipe tip 89 string "fringe" over band. Mark scallop points ½ in. above band edge, measuring 2¾ in. wide. Pipe tip 104 ruffles ¼ in. below scallop mark, extending center of ruffle ½ in. below top edge of band. Pipe tip 16 zigzag garlands at scallop marks. Position flowers at scallop points; pipe tip 3 dots. Imprint small "C" scroll pattern press, 1 in. apart, around top edge of cake. Pipe tip 16 scrolls over imprint; add tip 16 upright shells at opening of scrolls; add tip 16 star at base of shell. Pipe tip 16 shell "heart" at bottom of scrolls.

For 9 in. cake: repeat same "C" scroll pattern process as on 15 in. cake. Position drop flowers below scrolls. Add tip 18 reverse shell bottom border.

Pipe tip 16 scallops at edge of bottom 11 in. Heart Plate.

At reception: Position pillars, ornament and bowl with greenery. Attach pearl beads to edge of foil-wrapped board..

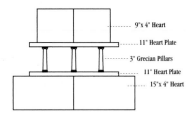

9"x 4" Heart
11" Heart Plate
3" Grecian Pillars
11" Heart Plate
15"x 4" Heart

CAKE ORNAMENTS

1. FOREVERMORE
Enchanting Art Plas couple adrift on a double-pleated ruffle which echoes the bride's rose motif. Graceful lucite-look backdrop carries a flowing floral arch with "pearl" loops.
Height: 10 ½ in.
Base: 4 ¾ in. diameter.
Black Tux
110-D-860
White Tux/Black Trousers
110-D-859

2. RIBBON DELIGHT
Swells of shimmering satin-edged ribbon unfurl at the base and in a heart shape behind our blissful Art Plas couple. "Pearl"-trimmed satin bows complete the sparkling look.
Height: 10 in.
Base: 4 ½ in. diameter.
Black Tux
110-D-932

3. NEW BEGINNING
Intertwined "pearl" arch frames our glamorous Art Plas couple amidst sprays of tulle. Delicate flowers and "pearl" petals add a light and airy touch above a base encircled by a double ruffle and "pearl" band. An excellent value.
Height: 10 in.
Base: 4 ½ x 6 in. oval.
Black Tux
110-D-858

4. ROSE GARDEN
A glorious floral arch of roses, ribbons and "pearl" sprays frame a loving porcelain bisque couple.
Height: 11 in.
Base: 4 ½ x 6 in. oval.
Black Tux
118-D-475

5. BEAUTIFUL
Joyous porcelain bisque couple in a mist of tulle, "pearl" leaves, flowers and lace. On a base of leaves trimmed in "pearls".
Height: 7 ½ in.
Base: 4 ½ x 6 in. oval.
Black Tux
118-D-445

6. TIMELESS
A radiant porcelain bisque couple under a lattice arch of "pearls". Adorned with lovely floral and "pearl" bursts on a lace and "pearl"-trimmed base.
Height: 10 in.
Base: 4 ½ x 6 in. oval.
Black Tux
118-D-455

Designer Series by
Ellen Williams

7. OUR DANCE
Graceful couple dances under an arched heart frame trimmed with lace. Floral blooms top the lace-edged base.
Height: 9 1/4 in.
Base: 4 1/2 x 6 in. oval.
Black Tux
118-D-650

8. ROMANTIC MOMENTS
Lily of the valley spray cascading from an opulent pillar frames the dancing couple. Pearl loops, leaves and lace add the finishing touches.
Height: 10 1/2 in.
Base: 4 1/2 x 6 in. oval.
White Couple/Black Tux
118-D-651

9. ALLURE
An enchanting gazebo wrapped with ivory tulle and prettied by a profusion of satin bows. White and ivory flowers enhance this lovely wedding setting. Exquisitely detailed Art Plas couples.
Height: 11 in.
Base: 5 in. diameter.
White Couple/Black Tux
101-D-1783
Ethnic Couple/Black Tux
101-D-1785

10. I DO
Double crystal-look hearts and bells highlighted with blossoms, satin ribbons, "pearls", ivory and white floral accents. Features painstakingly detailed Art Plas couples.
Height: 9 in.
Base: 4 1/2 in. diameter.
Ethnic Couple/Black Tux
101-D-1781
White Couple/Black Tux
101-D-1779

11. GARDEN DELIGHT
Breathtaking spiral holds a topiary of blooms and long streamers of ribbons and "pearls" accenting lovely detailed Art Plas couples. Crystal-look backdrop adds drama to the scene.
Height: 10 in.
Base: 4 3/4 in. diameter.
White Couple/Black Tux
101-D-1775
Ethnic Couple/Black Tux
101-D-1777

12. DEDICATION
A trio of chapel windows provides the inspiring backdrop for our magnificent Art Plas Our Day couple. Clusters of roses and bursts of tulle sweep above a band of openwork lace at the base.
Height: 7 in.
Base: 4 1/2 x 6 in. oval.
Black Tux
101-D-150

7.

8.

9.

10.

11.

12.

CAKE ORNAMENTS

1. **NEW** **PETITE COUNTRY & WESTERN**
Whimsical representation of a country kind of love. Art Plas figurine accented with lace, fabric roses and lasso!
Height: 7 in.
Base: 5 in. diameter.
White Couple/ White Tux
104-D-112

2-3. EXPRESSION OF LOVE
Our linked hearts float behind majestic Art Plas couples adrift in a trail of soft flowers and feather-edge ribbon. A "pearl"-trimmed lace band and ruffled lace at the base complete the romantic scene.
Height: 7 3/4 in.
Base: 4 1/2 in. diameter.
2. Ethnic Couple/Black Tux
101-D-933
3. White Couple/Black Tux
101-D-931

4. SWEETNESS
Entwined crystal-look hearts arise from a bounty of tulle surrounding our poised Art Plas couple. Tastefully trimmed with "pearl" accented satin bows, it's a fresh look at an outstanding value.
Height: 7 3/4 in.
Base: 4 1/2 in. diameter.
White Couple/Black Tux
101-D-153

5. EVERLASTING
A dramatic "pearl"-trimmed gazebo is the setting for this dainty porcelain couple. Tulle sprays tied with ribbons and flowing lily of the valley.
Height: 11 1/2 in.
Base: 5 in. diameter.
Black Tux
118-D-505

6. PETITE DELICATE JOY
Solitary petite porcelain bisque couple on a lacy ruffled base dotted with floral blooms and streamers.
Height: 6 in.
Base: 3 1/4 in. diameter.
Black Tux
108-D-645

Designer Series by

Ellen Williams

7. PETITE ROMANCE
Petite couple stands atop a base beautifed with gathered bows and streamers of feather edge and smooth edge ribbon.
Height: 5 1/4 in. Base: 3 1/4 in. diameter.
White Couple/Black Tux
104-D-942
White Couple/White Tux/White Trousers
104-D-941

8. PETITE RIBBON DELIGHT
Shimmering satin-edged ribbon heart frames our petite Art Plas couple. Enhanced with ribbon and "pearl" trim.
Height: 7 1/4 in. Base: 3 1/4 in. diameter.
White Couple/Black Tux   104-D-934
Ethnic Couple/Black Tux   104-D-936

9. PETITE HEART OF FANCY
Lovely lacy heart crested with a lavish bow and "pearl" ring is a fine backdrop for our petite Art Plas couple.
Height: 7 in. Base: 3 1/4 in. diameter.
Black Tux   104-D-932

10. PETITE LACE TRELLIS
Cameo-patterned lace arch encircles our petite couples. Lavishly adorned with ribbon bow and "pearl" trim.
Height: 7 1/2 in. Base: 3 1/4 in. diameter.
Ethnic Couple/Black Tux   104-D-940
White Couple/Black Tux   104-D-938

© 1991, 1992, 1993 EHW Enterprises, Inc.
Licensee Wilton Enterprises, Inc.

11. NATURAL BEAUTY
Lovebirds beneath filigree heart trimmed with lily of the valley and a smooth satin bow.
Height: 6 in. Base: 3 1/4 in. diameter.
White
106-D-1163

12. PETITE BELLS OF JOY
Cluster of white filigree bells with fabric roses, lace-covered arches and tulle.
Height: 7 in. Base: 3 1/4 in. diameter.
White
106-D-2658

13. LA BELLE PETITE
Tolling bell surrounded by tulle and flowers glimmers with iridescence.
Height: 5 1/2 in. Base: 3 1/4 in. diameter.
White
106-D-248

14. PETITE SPRING SONG
A dainty song bird duet arched in flowers, "pearls" and tulle.
Height: 7 in. Base: 3 1/4 in. diameter.
White
106-D-159

15. PETITE DOUBLE RING
Graceful doves land on simple wedding bands on heart base. Adorned with tulle puff.
Height: 5 1/2 in. Base: 3 1/4 in. diameter.
White
106-D-4316

CAKE ORNAMENTS

Designer Series by

Ellen Williams

1. SIMPLE JOYS
A trio of blooming roses, exquisite lace and "pearl" wisps decorate this simply beautiful ornament. Glorified by interlocked crystal-look hearts.
Height: 8 in. Base: $4\frac{1}{2}$ in. diameter.
103-D-150

2. OPULENCE
"Pearl"-adorned wedding bands shimmer on a base of "pearl" leaves and accordion-pleated lace.
Height: $6\frac{1}{2}$ in. Base: $4\frac{1}{2}$ in. diameter.
103-D-420

3. TRUE LOVE
"Pearl"-embellished swooning doves rest on a pair of "pearl" studded wedding bands. Tufts of tulle and soft roses complete the vision.
Height: $8\frac{1}{2}$ in. Base: $4\frac{5}{8}$ in. diameter.
103-D-410

4. CROWNING GLORY
Two fluttering doves alight on a lace and "pearl" trimmed heart and satiny bell. Lace also underscores the base.
Height: $9\frac{1}{2}$ in. Base: $4\frac{5}{8}$ in. diameter.
103-D-405

5. INSPIRATION
The gilded cross is highlighted on a petal base flowing with tulle bursts. A soft bouquet of posies drapes cross and base.
Height: $6\frac{1}{2}$ in. Base: $3\frac{1}{4}$ in. diameter.
106-D-355

6. MASTERPIECE
Ornately-trimmed bells toll out the happiest of wedding messages. Tied with ribbon and set in a lace-trimmed heart.
Height: $9\frac{1}{2}$ in. Base: $4\frac{1}{2}$ in. diameter.
Ivory   103-D-425
White   103-D-430

7. EXUBERANCE
Two graceful swans float on a lace-trimmed base. Both glide under a shower of flowing tulle and "pearl" decked buds.
Height: 7 in. Base: $4\frac{7}{8}$ in. diameter
103-D-440

8. 25TH & 50TH ANNIVERSARY ORNAMENTS
Lovely mementos from the Designer Series by Ellen Williams.
Height: 6 in. Base: $3\frac{1}{4}$ in. diameter.
50th Gold 105-D-4310

Not shown , but also available:
25th Silver 105-D-4300

NOTE: Some products offered in this publication may not be available in Canada.

1. LUSTROUS LOVE

Bursts of tulle peek from behind lace leaves; dotted with forget-me-nots and rimmed with gleaming "pearls". Satiny roses bloom while "pearls" are suspended on transparent strings around the happy glazed porcelain couple.
Height: 8 in. Base: 4 ⁵/₈ in. diameter
White 117-D-621

2. DEVOTION

Crystal-look arch is framed with gathered tulle and lace. Glazed porcelain couple stands on pedestal base in burst of tulle, blooms and "pearl" strands.
Height: 9¹/₂ in. Base: 4³/₄ in. diameter.
White 117-D-425

3. PROMISE

Simple beauty. Dramatic crystal-look heart frames dainty porcelain couple. Crystal-look base is covered with tulle, ribbons and fabric flowers.
Height: 9⁵/₈ in. Base: 4¹/₂ in. diameter.
White 117-D-315

4. REFLECTIONS

Sleek, streamlined and sophisticated. Dramatic crystal-look backdrop reflects porcelain couple, tulle burst, "pearl" sprays and florals.
Height: 8 in. Base: 4³/₄ in. diameter.
White 117-D-268

5. ECSTASY

Sprays of flowers and leaves surround a romantic porcelain pair. Delicate tulle forms a lovely base.
Height: 9¹/₂ in. Base: 4³/₄ in. diameter.
White 117-D-831

6. GARDEN ROMANCE

Charming porcelain couple stands in a gazebo decked with flowery vines. Clusters of tulle and ribbons complete this romantic hideaway.
Height: 10¹/₂ in. Base: 5 in. diameter.
White Iridescent 117-D-711

7. SPLENDID

Sweeping crystal-look curve surrounds adoring glazed porcelain pair. Cylindrical vase holds a matching spray of flowers that accents base. Add real flowers if you wish.
Height: 10¹/₂ in. Base: 4³/₄ in. diameter.
White 117-D-506

CAKE ORNAMENTS

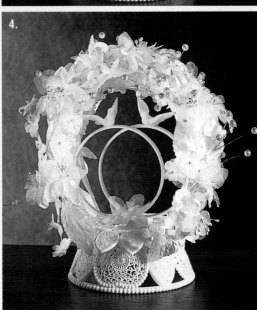

1. LACE CHARM
Luxuriant ruffled lace heart and base display the shimmering wedding bells. "Pearl" sprays and flowers add the final touches.
Height: 11 in.
Base: 4 3/4 in. diameter.
103-D-151

2. SWEET CEREMONY
Seed pearl heart frames glitter bell accented with tulle. Bell surrounds our classic couple.
Height: 10 in.
Base: 4 5/8 in. diameter.
Black Coat
101-D-22011

3. SPRING SONG
Perching lovebirds sing their romantic songs in a garden of posies and tulle.
Height: 9 1/2 in.
Base: 4 5/8 in. diameter.
111-D-2802

4. CIRCLES OF LOVE
Symbolic double rings and doves in a hideaway of flowers and "pearl" sprays.
Height: 10 in.
Base: 4 5/8 in. diameter.
White
103-D-9004

5. VICTORIAN CHARM
Graceful ribbon loops and fantasy florals layer over romantic satin five-bell cluster.
Height: 7 1/2 in.
Base: 4 1/2 in. diameter.
Ivory
103-D-1586

6. HEARTS TAKE WING
Romantic beak-to-beak birds perched on a setting of heart-shaped branches and tulle.
Height: 10 1/2 in.
Base: 4 1/2 in. diameter.
103-D-6218

NOTE: Some products offered in this publication may not be available in Canada.

94

1. LOVE ENDURES
Celebrate the years gone by with an opulent burst of glitter-edged tulle and glimmering ribbon. Topped with the appropriate shimmering number.
Height: 7¹/₂ in. Base: 4⁵/₈ in. diameter.
50th 102-D-151
25th 102-D-150

2. 25 OR 50 YEARS OF HAPPINESS
In gold or silver, the number tells the happy story. Accented with blooms and shimmering leaves.
Height: 10 in. Base: 4⁵/₈ in. diameter.
50th 102-D-223
Not shown , but also available:
25th 102-D-207

3. GOLDEN/SILVER JUBILEE
Celebrate the years with gold or silver flowers. Couple stands before numeral wreath with orchids, ferns and puffs of tulle.
Height: 8¹/₂ in. Base: 4⁵/₈ in. diameter.
Silver 102-D-1225
Not shown , but also available:
Gold 102-D-1250

4. PETITE DOUBLE RING DEVOTION
Celebrating couple surrounded by rings and the shimmer of "pearls" and ferns.
Height: 5 in. Base: 3¹/₄ in. diameter.
50th Gold 105-D-4605
Not shown , but also available:
25th Silver 105-D-4613

5. PETITE ANNIVERSARY YEARS
Beautiful blooms, leaves and sprays of tulle add appeal to this versatile favorite. Embossed wreath holds snap-on numbers to mark the milestones—5, 10, 15, 20, 40.
Height: 5³/₄ in. Base: 3¹/₄ in. diameter.
105-D-4257

6. PETITE ANNIVERSARY
Shining numeral wreath is highlighted by two fluttering doves.
Height: 5¹/₂ in. Base: 3¹/₄ in. diameter.
25th 105-D-4265
Not shown , but also available:
50th 105-D-4273

Designer Series by
Ellen Williams

7. JOYFUL DEBUT ORNAMENT WITH LA QUINCEAÑERA
Lavish lace, ribbon and "pearls" encircle the lovely young lady in celebration of her 15th birthday. Art Plas.
Height: 9 in. Base: 4⁵/₈ in. diameter.
203-D-306

8. LA QUINCEAÑERA FIGURINE
Sweetly posed Art Plas figurine is a beautiful remembrance of her 15th birthday jubilee. Lovely bridesmaid as well.
Height: 4¹/₂ in.
203-D-305

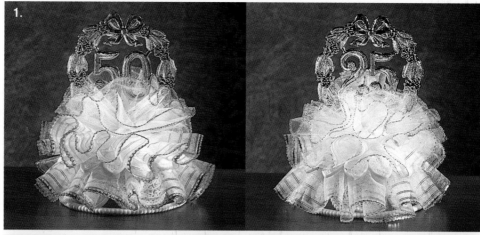

1.

2.

3.

4.

5.

6.

7.

8.

ACCESSORIES

On your special day, the details make all the difference.
Loving Traditions™ perfects the little touches that make memories
. . . a complete selection of lace-lavished keepsakes.

Loving
TRADITIONS™

1. CAKE KNIFE & SERVER
Gleaming stainless with acrylic handles. Tied with sprays of flowers, ribbons and "pearls".
Cake Knife 120-D-704
Cake Server 120-D-705
2 Pc. Knife & Server Set 120-D-703

2-3. 2 PC. FLUTED GLASSES SETS
Rosebud motif; trimmed with lace and ribbon. Spiral stem. 2 glasses per set. Height: 8 3/8 in.
2. Bride & Groom Set 120-D-708
3. Anniversary Set 120-D-707

4-5. 2 PC. TOASTING GLASSES SETS
Lillies of the valley design with satin ribbons. 2 glasses per set. Height: 4 1/2 in.
4. Bride & Groom Set 120-D-203
5. Anniversary Set 120-D-205

6. UNITY CANDLE
Intricately carved pastel candle features ring-bearing doves.
9 in. high x 2 3/4 in. diameter.
120-D-710

7. **NEW** BOUQUET OF LACE UNITY CANDLE
Appliqués of lacy roses sparked with iridescence decorate this symbol of love. 9 in. high x 2 3/4 in. diameter.
120-D-711

8. **NEW** VICTORIAN LACE UNITY CANDLE
Lace motif surrounds this eternal flame. 9 in. high x 2 3/4 in. diam.
120-D-712

9. **NEW** 2 PC. VICTORIAN LACE TAPER CANDLE SET
10. in ivory candles punctuated with pearlized roses. Ideal with Candlelight Cake Stand, p. 108.
120-D-722

10. PLUME PEN
A signature touch of romance.
120-D-804

11. GUEST BOOK
An elegant keepsake engraved with gold-leaf lettering.
120-D-800

12. BRIDE'S GARTERS
Lacy satin band trimmed with ribbons and "pearls", featuring a generous use of lace. Wide elastic band for comfort.
Blue   120-D-402
Pink   120-D-400
White   120-D-401
Ivory   120-D-403
Black   120-D-404

13. RING BEARER'S PILLOWS
Elegant, shimmery satin hand-made pillows in two popular shapes. Trimmed with delicate lace, ribbon, and "pearls". Square pillows approx 10 1/2 in.
Ribbon Square-White
120-D-104
Ribbon Heart-White
120-D-100
Lacy Square-Ivory   120-D-107
Lacy Square-White 120-D-106

Bomboniere!®
Party Favors

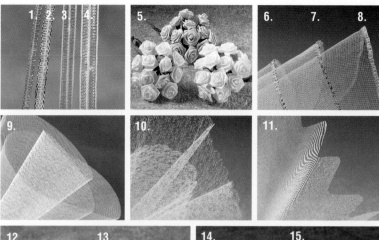

1-4. INSTANT BOW RIBBON
Woven-in pull strings help you create foolproof, perfectly-shaped iridescent bows in colors that complement every party theme. Each yard makes one bow.

1. $^3/_{16}$ in. Gold   1003-D-3204   10 yard spool
2. $^5/_{16}$ in. White   1003-D-3240   8 yard spool
3. $^5/_{16}$ in. Pink   1003-D-3252   8 yard spool
4. $^5/_{16}$ in. Blue   1003-D-3246   8 yard spool

5. RIBBON ROSES
Lifelike, beautiful blooms on wired stems are easy to insert in all styles of favors. Pretty on packages too!

Pink   1006-D-85   White   1006-D-84
Blue   1006-D-86   pk. of 12

TULLE CIRCLES
Sheer mesh fabric for elegant puffs and pleated bows. 9 in. diameter.

6-8. LUREX-EDGE TULLE CIRCLES
6. Silver   1005-D-22   7. Gold   1005-D-21
8. Iridescent   1005-D-20   pk. of 12

9. WHITE TULLE CIRCLES
1005-D-1   pk. of 25

10. LACE SCALLOPED-EDGE TULLE CIRCLES
White   1005-D-24   pk. of 25

11. ORGANZA SCALLOPED-EDGE TULLE CIRCLES
White   1005-D-23   pk. of 12

12. TUXEDO BOXES   4 in.
1006-D-48   pk. of 2

13. TOP HAT AND CANE   1 in. hat; 4 in. long cane.
1006-D-11   pk. of 2

14. FILIGREE HEART BOXES   2$^1/_4$ in..
1006-D-21   pk. of 4

15. ROUND BASKETS   3 in. high   1006-D-113   pk. of 4

16. FLOWER CARTS   4$^1/_2$ in.   1006-D-24   pk. of 2

17. PARTY PARASOLS   2$^3/_4$ In..   1006-D-27   pk. of 4

18. WEDDING COUPLE WITH GREY TUXEDO
1$^7/_8$ in.   1006-D-14

19. WEDDING COUPLE WITH BLACK TUXEDO
2$^1/_2$ in.   1006-D-25

20. LACE BONNET   4$^1/_4$ in. wide.
1006-D-51

21. SATIN HEART PILLOW   3$^1/_4$ in. .
1006-D-26   pk. of 2

22. PEARL SWANS   3 in.
1006-D-108   pk. of 4

23. CHAMPAGNE GLASSES   2 in.
Silver   1006-D-103   pk. of 4
Clear   1006-D-105   pk. of 4

24. HEART TAGS   3$^1/_2$ x 1 in. .
1006-D-44   pk. of 12

25. ANNIVERSARY BANDS $^3/_4$ in. diameter.
Gold   1006-D-19   pk. of 12   Silver   1006-D-20   pk. of 12
Gold   1006-D-100   pk. of 48   Silver   1006-D-101   pk. of 48

26. "PEARL" HEARTS   4$^1/_2$ in.
1006-D-35   pk. of 6

27. "PEARL" SPRAYS   4 sprays of 3; 5$^1/_4$ in.
1006-D-31   pk. of 12

28. STAMENS   3 in.
1006-D-30   pk. of 12

Bomboniere!® products are both imported and made in the United States.

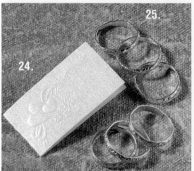

FIGURINES

1. A DAY TO REMEMBER ♪
Revolving musical ornament plays "Waltz of the Flowers". Supremely detailed with floral embellishments. Height: 8 in. Base: 4 1/2 in.
White Couple/Black Tux   215-D-410

2. SWEET SYMPHONY* ♪
Musical plays "The Wedding March". Hand-painted, detailed Art Plas. Height: 7 3/4 in. Base: 3 1/2 in. diam.
Black Tux   215-D-776

3. 🔘NEW PETITE COUNTRY & WESTERN
Lighthearted tribute when country folk wed! Detailed and crafted in Art Plas. Height: 4 in.
214-D-1120

4. LOVE'S DUET
Captivating detail enhances this elegant Art Plas figure. Height: 6 in.
Black Tux   202-D-402
White Tux   202-D-403

5. 🔘NEW ETHNIC LOVE'S DUET
Romantic ethnic Art Plas couple complements cake designs with grace and beauty. Height: 6 in.
Black Tux   202-D-412

6. TOGETHER FOREVER*
Romantic porcelain couple in a traditional bridal pose. Height: 6 1/2 in.
Black Tux/White Dress   214-D-415

7. PETITE TOGETHER FOREVER*
Porcelain figure is perfect for cakes and table decoration. Height: 4 1/2 in.
Black Tux   214-D-439

8. FIRST DANCE
Beautifully defined and detailed enchanted Art Plas couple capture the moment of their first dance. Height: 6 in.
Black Tux   202-D-411
White Tux   202-D-410

9. OUR DAY
Adoring Art Plas bride and groom in a striking natural pose. Height: 4 1/2 in.
Black Tux   202-D-409

10. HAPPIEST DAY
Sweetly poised ethnic couple with life-like Art Plas bouquets and headpiece. Height: 4 1/2 in.
Black Tux   202-D-306
White Tux/White Trousers   202-D-305

11. PETITE HAPPIEST DAY
Graceful ethnic Art Plas couple ideal for cakes and place settings. Height: 3 1/2 in.
Black Tux   202-D-404

12. LASTING LOVE
Lovely bride has a flowing tulle veil. Made of life-like Art Plas material. Height: 4 1/2 in.
White Tux/White Trousers   202-D-303
Black Tux   202-D-302

13. PETITE LASTING LOVE
Our petite rendition with all the beautiful Art Plas detail intact. Height: 3 1/2 in.
Black Tux   202-D-401
White Tux/White Trousers   202-D-400

15. DESIGNER BRIDESMAIDS

So many beautiful jewel and soft tones match many color themes. Art Plas. Height: 4¹/₂ in.

NEW Ivory	203-D-9122	pk. of 2
NEW Blush	203-D-9123	pk. of 2
Black	203-D-9110	pk. of 2
Raspberry (fuchsia)	203-D-9108	pk. of 2
Dark Pink	203-D-9119	pk. of 2
White	203-D-9111	pk. of 2
Sapphire (dark blue)	203-D-9109	pk. of 2
Emerald (dark green)	203-D-9104	pk. of 2
Amethyst (purple)	203-D-9107	pk. of 2

16. ETHNIC DESIGNER BRIDESMAIDS

Bridesmaids dressed in a beautiful variety of shades that will coordinate well with many wedding color motifs. Art Plas. Height: 4¹/₂ in.

NEW Ivory	203-D-9120	pk. of 2
NEW Blush	203-D-9121	pk. of 2
White	203-D-9114	pk. of 2

17. DESIGNER GROOMSMEN

Handsome groomsmen in attractive matte finish. Art Plas. Height: 4¹/₂ in.

| Black Tux | 203-D-9101 | pk. of 2 |
| White Coat | 203-D-9100 | pk. of 2 |

18. ETHNIC DESIGNER GROOMSMEN

Groomsmen have the option of exactly matching their tuxedo to that of the groom. Art Plas. Height 4¹/₂ in.

| Black Tux | 203-D-9116 | pk. of 2 |
| White Coat | 203-D-9117 | pk. of 2 |

19. RING BEARER

Charming young man carries a gold trimmed pillow and shimmering rings. Highly detailed cake decoration and keepsake. Height: 3¹/₄ in.
203-D-7887

20. FLOWER GIRL

Exquisitely detailed down to her shimmering dress and floral basket. Perfect cake decoration and memento of the occasion. Height: 3¹/₄ in.
203-D-7879

21. ANY ANNIVERSARY & 25TH DESIGNER COUPLE

Precious keepsakes from the Designer Series by Ellen Williams. Height: 4¹/₂ in.

Any Anniversary Ivory
203-D-1850
25th Silver   203-D-1825

© 1991, 1992, 1995 EHW Enterprises, Inc.,
Licensee Wilton Enterprises

22. ANNIVERSARY COUPLE

Gold or silver gown. Plastic. Height: 3¹/₂ in.
50th Gold   203-D-1821
25th Silver 203-D-2828

23. STYLIZED COUPLE

Glazed porcelain couple. Height: 4⁵/₈ in.
202-D-218

24. LIBERATED BRIDE

A light-hearted approach! Plastic. Height: 4¹/₂ in.
2113-D-4188

25. RELUCTANT GROOM

Don't let this one get away! Plastic. Height: 4¹/₂ in.
1316-D-9520

26. CLASSIC COUPLE

Designed in plastic. Height: 4¹/₂ in.
Black Tux   202-D-8110

ACCENTS & ACCESSORIES

1. 14 PC. ARCHED TIER SET

Quite dramatic when used with Kolor-Flo Fountain. Includes: Six 13 in. arched columns, two super strong 18 in. round Decorator Preferred Separator Plates and six angelic cherubs to attach to columns with royal icing or glue. See our Gazebo Cake Kit (page 102) that works beautifully with Arched Pillars.
301-D-1982   set

Be prepared with replacement pieces for the Arched Tier Set:

18 in. Decorator Preferred Plate
302-D-18

13 in. Arched Pillars
303-D-9719

SAVE on pack of six Arched Pillars.
301-D-9809   pk. of 6

2. 6 PC. HARVEST CHERUB SEPARATOR SET

Includes four 7 in. Harvest Cherub pillars, two 9 in. separator plates (lower plate has 12 in. overall diameter).
301-D-3517   set

3. DANCING CUPID PILLARS

This charming character is wonderful on wedding shower or Valentine cakes.
$5^1/_2$ in. high.
303-D-1210   pk. of 4

4. CHERUB SNAP-ONS

Accent 5 and 7 in. Grecian pillars. (Pillars not included.) $3^1/_2$ in. high.
305-D-4104   pk. of 4

5. FROLICKING CHERUB

Animated character. 5 in. high.
1001-D-244

6. ANGEL DUET

Fluttering fancies. A pair per package.
$2^1/_2$ x 2 in.
1001-D-457   pk. of 2

7. MUSICAL TRIO

Setting just the right mood.
Each 3 in. high.
1001-D-368   pk. of 3

8. KNEELING CHERUB FOUNTAIN

Beautiful when accented with tinted piping gel and flowers. 4 in. high.
1001-D-9380

9. ANGELINOS

Heavenly addition to wedding, birthday and holiday cakes. 2 x 3 in.
1001-D-504   pk. of 6

10. CHERUB CARD HOLDER

What neat place markers, too. (Cards not included.) $1^5/_8$ x $3^3/_8$ in.
1001-D-9374   pk. of 4

11. HEAVENLY HARPISTS

Striking the perfect chord.
$3^1/_2$ in. high.
1001-D-7029   pk. of 4

NOTE: Some products offered in this publication may not be available in Canada.

ACCENTS & ACCESSORIES

1. WHITE PEARL BEADING

With just one continuous row of lustrous pearls you can transform a beautiful cake into a glorious work of art. Stunning and easy to work with, these pearls are a must for all serious decorators. Molded on one continuous 5 yard strand, they can be easily cut to size. **To use:** Work with long, continuous strands. Position before icing crusts. Trim after pearls are in position to insure exact measure. Do not trim smaller than 6 in. lengths. Remove pearls before cutting and serving cake.

Size	Stock No.
6 mm	211-D-1990
4 mm	211-D-1989

2. FLORAL PUFF ACCENT

5 1/2 in. tulle puff with soft flowers and "pearl" sprays.
White 211-D-1011

3. PEARL LEAF PUFF

5 1/2 in. tulle puff with "pearls".
White 211-D-1125

4. KISSING LOVE BIRDS

Beak-to-beak romantics. 5 1/2 in. high
1002-D-206

5. PETITE SONG BIRDS

A note of grace and poise. 2 1/4 in.
1316-D-1210 pk. of 4

6. LOVE DOVES

Devoted duo provides the perfect finish. 4 x 2 3/4 in.
1002-D-1806 pk. of 2

7. SMALL DOVES

Elegant atop cakes or favors. 2 x 1 1/2 in.
1002-D-1710 pk. of 12

8. GLITTERED DOVES

2 x 1 1/2 in. Coated with non-edible glitter.
1006-D-166 pk. of 12

9. FLOWER SPIKES

Fill with water, push into cake, add flowers. 3 in. high.
1008-D-408 pk. of 12

10. ARTIFICIAL LEAVES

Green or white cloth; gold or silver foil. 1 7/8 in. and 1 1/4 in. sizes. (Add **1005-D-** prefix before number.)

Color	No. per pk.	1 7/8 in. Stock No.	1 1/4" in. Stock No.
Gold	144	6518	6712
Silver	144	6526	6720
Green	72	7555	7570
White	72	7565	N/A

11. PEARL LEAVES 2 1/4 in. long.
211-D-1201 $2.99 pk. of 2

12. FILIGREE BELLS* Beautiful floral detail.

Height	Stock No.	# Per Pk.
1 in.	1001-D-9447	12
1 7/8 in.	1001-D-9422	6
2 1/4 in.	1001-D-9439	6

13. GLITTERED BELLS*

A shimmering addition.

Height	Stock No.	# Per Pk.
1 in.	1007-D-9061	12
1 7/8 in.	1007-D-9088	6

14. OPENWORK BELLS* 1 3/4 in. high.
1006-D-10 pk. of 6

15. WHITE FROSTED BELLS* 5/8 in. high.
1006-D-36 pk. of 6

* Ribbon not included.

CAUTION: Contains small parts. Not recommended for use by children 3 years and under

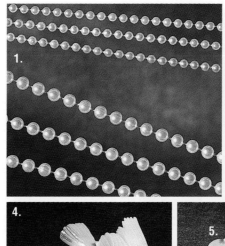

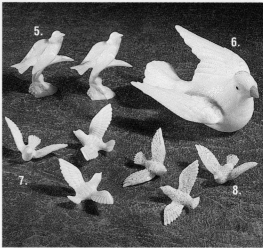

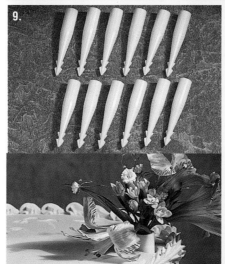

ACCENTS & ACCESSORIES

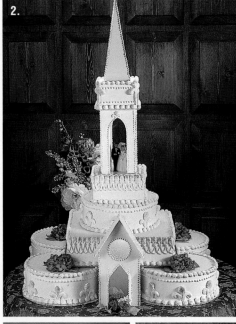

1. 20 PC. GAZEBO CAKE KIT
The delicate cuts and trellis-work openings of the twenty arch and trellis pieces in this kit are accomplished with a laser. The paper is coated and remarkably sturdy. Complete assembly instructions included. For use only with: two 10 in. Wilton Separator Plates and four 6 1/2 in. Wilton Arched Pillars (top layer); and two 18 in. Wilton Separator Plates and six 13 in. Wilton Arched Pillars (bottom layer). Pillars and plates sold separately (p 106-107).
2104-D-350 kit

2. 10 PC. CATHEDRAL CAKE KIT
Includes: 5 easy-to-assemble white church pieces, 4 white plastic cake supports, a church window that can be illuminated from within.
2104-D-2940 kit

3. CHAPEL WINDOWS
Refelective back window setting adds a glimmering effect. Use with Oval Base (shown below) or alone. Size: 6 1/2 x 5 x 1 in. deep.
205-D-3060

4. GAZEBO SET 5 x 9 in.
205-D-8298 set

5. SEED PEARL HEART 7 x 6 1/2 in.
205-D-1006 pk. of 3

6. FILIGREE HEART FRAMES
7 x 6 1/2 in.   205-D-1501 pk. of 3
4 x 4 in.   205-D-1527 pk. of 3

7. SCROLLS 2 3/4 x 1 1/4 in.
1004-D-2801 pk. of 24

8. LACY HEARTS 3 3/4 x 3 1/2 in.
1004-D-2306 pk. of 12

9. FILIGREE SWIRLS 4 x 2 1/4 in.
1004-D-2100 pk. of 12

10. CRYSTAL-LOOK HEARTS
5 1/2 in.   205-D-1674
4 1/4 in.   205-D-1672

11. DOUBLE WEDDING BANDS
3 1/2 in. diam.   201-D-1008

12. CRYSTAL-LOOK BOWL
4 1/2 in. diameter, 1 1/2 in. deep.
205-D-1404

13. IRIDESCENT GRAPES 2 x 2 in.
1099-D-200 pk. of 4

14. IRIDESCENT DOVES 2 in. wide.
1002-D-509 pk. of 6

15. CIRCLES OF LACE
Lacy alcove with tulle and a shimmery bell. Height: 10 in. Base: 4 5/8 in. diameter.
210-D-1986

16. FLORAL ARCH
Botanical arch covered with gleaming flowers. Height: 10 in. Base: 4 5/8 in. diam.
210-D-1987

17. ROMANTIC HEART BASE
2 pieces, 2 base sizes, both 1 1/2 in. high.
Base: 4 5/8 in. diameter.   201-D-7332
Base: 3 1/4 in. diameter.   201-D-7847

18. FLORAL BASE
White. Height: 1 1/2 in. Base: 4 7/8 in. diam.
201-D-1815

19. CRYSTAL-LOOK BASE
Height: 1 3/4 in. Base: 4 1/2 in. diameter.
201-D-1450

20. IVORY FLORAL SCROLL BASE
Height: 2 1/2 in. Base: 4 1/2 in. diameter.
White   201-D-1303
Ivory   201-D-305

21. OVAL BASE
Bead border. 4 1/2 x 6 in.
201-D-420

CAKE FOUNTAINS & STAIRWAYS

1. THE KOLOR-FLO FOUNTAIN

Present your elegant formal tiers in the most dramatic way with our colorful, shimmering waterfall. Water pours from three levels. Remove top levels for smaller fountain arrangement. Intricate light system with two bulbs for extra brilliance. Use with 14 in. or larger plates, 13 in. or taller pillars for tallest cascade. Coordinates with our Crystal-Look Tier Set, p. 105. Plastic fountain bowl is $9^3/_4$ in. diameter. 110-124 V, AC motor with 65 in. cord. Pumps water electrically. Directions and replacement part information included.
306-D-2599

Replacement Parts

Pump	306-D-1002
Piston	306-D-1029
Pump/Bulb Bracket	306-D-1037
Light Socket	306-D-1045
Light Bulb	306-D-1053
Cascade/Pump Connector	306-D-1088
Floater Switch	306-D-1096
Upper Cascade	306-D-1118
Middle Cascade	306-D-1126
Lower Cascade	306-D-1134
Bowl	306-D-1142
Bottom Base	306-D-1169

2. 4 PC. FOUNTAIN CASCADE SET

Dome shapes redirect water over their surface in nonstop streams. Set includes 4 pieces: $2^1/_2$ in., $4^1/_2$ in., 8 in. and $11^1/_2$ in. diam. (Kolor-Flo Fountain sold separately).
306-D-1172 set

3. FLOWER HOLDER RING

Put at base of Kolor-Flo Fountain.
Size: $12^1/_2$ in. diam. x 2 in. high. Plastic.
305-D-435

4. **NEW** FRESH FLOWER HOLDERS

Inserts easily under cake tiers to hold cascading blooms. greenery, pearl sprays, tulle puffs and more. Use with floral oasis to keep flowers looking fresh. $2^1/_4$ in. high with $1^1/_4$ in. well.
205-D-8500 pk. of 2

5. 3 PC. CRYSTAL BRIDGE AND GRACEFUL STAIRWAY SET

Create a dramatic masterpiece. Includes two stairways ($16^3/_4$ in. long) and one platform ($4^3/_4$ x 5 in.). Plastic.
205-D-2311 set
ONE STAIRWAY ONLY
205-D-2315

6. 3 PC. FILIGREE PLATFORM AND STAIRWAY SET

Bridge the gap between lavish tiers. Includes two stairways ($16^1/_4$ in. long) and one platform ($4^3/_4$ x 5 in.). Plastic.
205-D-2109 set
ONE STAIRWAY ONLY
205-D-1218

7. 24 PC. STAIRSTEPS SET

Twenty-four 1 in. high stairs snap together with 3 in. candleholders.
1107-D-8180 set

8. SUPER STRONG CAKE STAND

Holds up to 185 pounds of cake! High impact polystyrene and underweb of ribbing make stand super strong. Height: $2^3/_4$ in. Diameter: 18 in., to accommodate larger cakes.
307-D-1200

103

WEDDING CAKE STANDS

1. GARDEN CAKE STAND
An elegant way to present your cake. Its dramatic scrolls and rich wrought-iron look are inspired by the revival in metalwork – a style that's particularly lovely surrounded by greenery. Fast and easy to use – simply place cakes on plates and set on the stand. Painted metal stand is 23 in. high x 22 in. wide and uses any standard 10 in., 14 in. and 18 in. separator plates. Satellite garden stands sold individually below.
307-D-860

SATELLITE GARDEN CAKE STAND
Painted metal stand coordinates with garden cake stand above. Holds a 12 in. separator plate. Sold individually.
307-D-861
Separator Plates sold separately on page 107.

2. 🔵NEW CANDLELIGHT CAKE STAND
Updated look emphasizes swirls of beautiful scrollwork and hearts. Now reinforced with a crossbar for more support. Sturdy enameled metal design holds up to 40 lbs. Ideal for 3 stacked tiers supported by a 14 in. separator plate. Stand is $21^1/_2$ in. diam. ($13^1/_4$ in. center cake area) x 5 in. high and uses standard $^7/_8$ in. candles. Our taper candle set, shown on p. 96, is a perfect complement to this stand. (Plates and candles not included.)
307-D-871

3. 4 PC. FLOATING TIERS CAKE STAND SET
Display three tiers on this graceful metal cake stand. Fast and easy to use! Set includes 17 in. high stand and 8 in., 12 in. and 16 in. smooth separator plates and instructions.
307-D-825   set
Additional plates available.
(Same plates as Crystal-Clear Cake Divider Set).

Plate	Number
8 in.	302-D-9749
12 in.	302-D-9765
16 in.	302-D-9780

4. 30 PC. CRYSTAL-CLEAR CAKE DIVIDER SET
Plastic separator plates $^1/_2$ in. diameter x $7^1/_2$ in. high. Clear plastic twist legs penetrate cake and rest on plate (dowel rods not needed). Includes 6 in., 8 in., 10 in., 12 in., 14 in. and 16 in. plates plus 24 legs.
SAVE 25% ON SET   301-D-9450   set
Additional plates available.

Plate	Number	Plate	Number
6 in.	302-D-9730	12 in.	302-D-9765
8 in.	302-D-9749	14 in.	302-D-9773
10 in.	302-D-9757	16 in.	302-D-9780

$7^1/_2$ IN. TWIST LEGS   303-D-9794   pk. of 4

9 IN. TWIST LEGS   Add more height.
303-D-977 pk. of 4

5. 13 PC. TALL TIER STAND SET
Five twist-apart columns $6^1/_2$ in. high with 1 bottom and 1 top bolt; 18 in. footed base plate; 8 in., 10 in., 12 in., 14 in. and 16 in. separator plates (interchangeable, except footed base plate). Plastic.
SAVE 25% ON SET   304-D-7915   set
Additional plates and columns available.

Plate	Number	Plate	Number
8 in.	302-D-7894	14 in.	302-D-7940
10 in.	302-D-7908	16 in.	302-D-7967
12 in.	302-D-7924	18 in.	302-D-7983

Column	Number
$6^1/_2$ in.	303-D-7910
$7^3/_4$ in.	304-D-5009
$13^1/_2$ in.	303-D-703

TOP COLUMN CAP NUT   304-D-7923
GLUE-ON PLATE LEGS   304-D-7930
BOTTOM COLUMN BOLT   304-D-7941

6. TALL TIER 4-ARM BASE STAND
Replace Tall Tier Base Plate (see No. 5) with this heavy-duty plastic support; add separator plates up to 12 in. For proper balance, add up to 3 graduated tiers to center column. Includes base bolt.
304-D-8245
BASE BOLT ONLY   304-D-8253

7. CAKE CORER TUBE
Prepare tiers quickly and neatly for the Tall Tier Stand column. Serrated edge removes cake centers with one push. Ice cake before using. 7 in. long solid center fits into $6^1/_2$ in. long hollow corer to eject cake bits. Cleans easily.
304-D-8172
NOTE: Some products offered in this publication may not be available in Canada.

1. 54-PC. GRECIAN PILLAR AND PLATE SET

A deluxe money-saving collection for the serious cake decorator. Features Decorator Preferred scalloped-edge separator plates and 5 in. pillars. Includes: two each 6 in., 8 in., 10 in., 12 in. and 14 in. plates; 20 Grecian pillars and 24 pegs.

SAVE 22% ON SET
301-D-8380   set

2. 8 PC. SIX-COLUMN TIER SET

Includes six 13 ³/₄ in. Roman columns and two super strong 18-in. round Decorator Preferred Separator Plates. A lovely set to use with the Kolor-Flo Fountain (sold on p. 103). Plastic.
301-D-1981   set

3. 14 PC. ARCHED TIER SET

Quite dramatic when used with Kolor-Flo Fountain. (sold on p. 103) Includes: Six 13 in. arched columns, two super strong 18 in. round Decorator Preferred Separator Plates and six angelic cherubs to attach to columns with royal icing or glue. Recommended for use with Gazebo Wedding Cake Kit (sold on p. 102).
301-D-1982   set

4. 6 PC. CRYSTAL-LOOK TIER SET

The ideal style and height to work with the Kolor-Flo Fountain and a beautiful way to present any tiered cake. Plastic set includes two 17 in. plates; four 13 ³/₄ in. pillars.
301-D-1387   set

5. 6 PC. HARVEST CHERUB SEPARATOR SET

An idyllic setting for a most romantic cake. Pillars simply snap on to plates for strong support. Set includes four 7 in. Harvest Cherub pillars and two 9 in. separator plates (lower plate has 12 in. overall diameter).
301-D-3517   set

6. 10 PC. CLASSIC SEPARATOR SETS

Stately Grecian pillars and scalloped-edge plates create beautiful settings for all tiered cakes. Sets include 2 Decorator Preferred Plates, 4 pillars and 4 pegs.

6 IN. PLATE SET WITH 3 IN. PILLARS
2103-D-639   set

8 IN. PLATE SET WITH 5 IN. PILLARS
2103-D-256   set

10 IN. PLATE SET WITH 5 IN. PILLARS
2103-D-108   set

12 IN. PLATE SET WITH 5 IN. PILLARS
2103-D-124   set

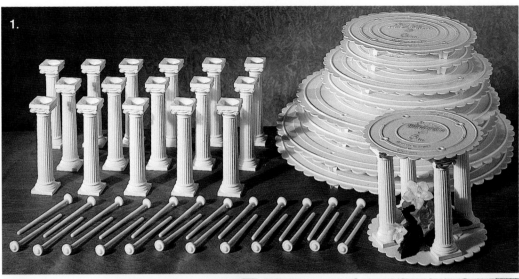

PILLARS & DOWELS

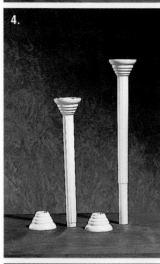

1. GRECIAN PILLARS
Elegantly scrolled and ribbed.
3 in. 303-D-3606 pk. of 4
5 in. 303-D-3703 pk. of 4
7 in. 303-D-3705 pk. of 4

2. GRECIAN SPIKED PILLARS
Eliminates need for separator plates on cake tier tops. Push into cake to rest on separator plate or cake circle beneath. Wide diameter bottom for increased stability.
5 in. 303-D-3708 pk. of 4
7 in. 303-D-3710 pk. of 4
9 in. 303-D-3712 pk. of 4

3. CRYSTAL-LOOK SPIKED PILLARS
Push into cake to rest on separator plate or cake circle beneath. Double cake circles for extra support.
7 in. 303-D-2322 pk. of 4
9 in. 303-D-2324 pk. of 4

4. DISPOSABLE PILLARS WITH RINGS
7 IN. PILLARS WITH RINGS
303-D-4000 pk. of 8 (4 each)
9 IN. PILLARS WITH RINGS
303-D-4001 pk. of 8 (4 each)

5. "HIDDEN" PILLARS
Designed to separate cake tiers slightly and create a floating illusion — adapted from the English method of cake decorating. Pushed into cake tiers as dowel rods, hidden pillars fit onto all white separator plates except Tall Tier. Trimmable, hollow plastic.
6 in. 303-D-8 pk. of 4

6. LATTICE COLUMNS
Flattering garden-inspired designs.
3 in. 303-D-2131 pk. of 4
5 in. 303-D-2151 pk. of 4
13 in. 303-D-2113 each

7. ARCHED PILLARS
Grecian-inspired with arched support.
4 1/2 in. 303-D-452 pk. of 4
6 1/2 in. 303-D-657 pk. of 4
13 in. 301-D-9809 pk. of 6

8. ROMAN COLUMNS
Handsome pillars may be used with Kolor-Flo Fountain.
10 1/4 in. 303-D-8135
13 3/4 in. 303-D-2129

9. CRYSTAL-LOOK PILLARS
Combine with crystal-look plates and Crystal Bridge and Stairway Set.
3 in. 303-D-2171 pk. of 4
5 in. 303-D-2196 pk. of 4
7 in. 303-D-2197 pk. of 4
*13 3/4 in. 303-D-2242
*(Use only with 17 in. crystal plate sold on p. 107.)

10. SWAN PILLARS
Grecian pillars with romantic swan bases add grace to your masterpiece. Height: 4 in.
303-D-7725 pk. of 4

11. SNAP-ON CHERUB
Accent 5, 7 in. Grecian pillars. 3 1/2 in. high.
305-D-4104 pk. of 4

12. DANCING CUPID PILLARS
Wedding shower, Valentine cakes. 5 1/2 in. high.
303-D-1210 pk. of 4

13. PLASTIC DOWEL RODS
Heavy-duty hollow plastic provides strong, sanitary support for all tiered cakes. Can be cut with serrated knife to desired length. Length: 12 3/4 in. Diameter: 3/4 in.
399-D-801 pk. of 4

14. WOODEN DOWEL RODS
Cut and sharpen with strong shears and knife. Length: 12 in. Diameter: 1/2 in.
399-D-1009 pk. of 12

15. PLASTIC PEGS
Insure that cake layers and separator plates atop cakes stay in place. These pegs do not add support, so dowel rod cake properly before using. Length: 4 in.
399-D-762 pk. of 12

Decorator Preferred®

- *Guaranteed Non-Breakable*
- *Circles of Strength Construction*
- *Lovely Scalloped Edges*
- *Easy Size Identification*
- *Smooth Back*

1. DECORATOR PREFERRED® SEPARATOR PLATES

Our best, strongest separator plates with the strength and beauty serious cake decorators require.

6 in.	302-D-6
7 in.	302-D-7
8 in.	302-D-8
9 in.	302-D-9
10 in.	302-D-10
11 in.	302-D-11
12 in.	302-D-12
13 in.	302-D-13
14 in.	302-D-14
15 in.	302-D-15
16 in.	302-D-16
18 in.	302-D-18

BAKER'S BEST®

2. DISPOSABLE SINGLE PLATES

Baker's Best® Disposable Separator Plates are the perfect option for busy decorators. Use these sturdy plates with pillars and adjustable pillar rings sold on page 106. All are made of recyclable plastic.

6 in. Plate	302-D-4000
7 in. Plate	302-D-4001
8 in. Plate	302-D-4002
9 in. Plate	302-D-4003
10 in. Plate	302-D-4004
12 in. Plate	302-D-4006
14 in. Plate	302-D-4008

3. CRYSTAL-LOOK PLATES

Use with crystal-look pillars sold on p. 106.

7 in.	302-D-2013
9 in.	302-D-2035
11 in.	302-D-2051
13 in.	302-D-2078
*17 in.	302-D-1810

*(Use only with 13 $^3/_4$ in. crystal pillars)

4. HEART SEPARATOR PLATES

8 in.	302-D-2112
11 in.	302-D-2114
14 $^1/_2$ in.	302-D-2116
16 $^1/_2$ in.	302-D-2118

5. OVAL SEPARATOR PLATES

8 $^1/_2$ x 6 in.	302-D-2130
11 $^1/_2$ x 8 $^1/_2$ in.	302-D-2131
14 $^1/_2$ x 8 $^1/_2$ in.	302-D-2132

6. SQUARE SEPARATOR PLATES

7 in.	302-D-1004
9 in.	302-D-1020
11 in.	302-D-1047
13 in.	302-D-1063

7. HEXAGON SEPARATOR PLATES

7 in.	302-D-1705
10 in.	302-D-1748
13 in.	302-D-1764
16 in.	302-D-1799

1. GUARANTEED NON-BREAKABLE!

2.

3.

4.

5.

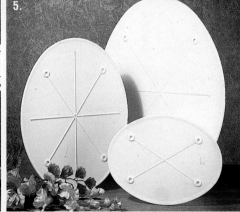

6.

7.

FRESH FLOWERS & ACCESSORIES

THE MAGIC OF CANDLELIGHT

Unforgettable — your wedding cake basking in the glow of our updated candlelight cake stand. Redesigned for a more romantic look, with an abundance of graceful scrollwork that works beautifully with arrangements of flowers and greenery. Our new wire lace collection of accents perfectly complements this beautifully scrolled stand . . . delicate openwork designs to enhance any wedding cake.

1. NEW CANDLELIGHT CAKE STAND
Updated look emphasizes swirls of beautiful scrollwork. Now reinforced with a crossbar for more support. Sturdy enameled metal design holds up to 40 lbs. Ideal for 3 stacked tiers supported by a 14 in. separator plate. Stand is 21 1/2 in. diam. (13 1/4 in. center cake area) x 5 in high and uses standard 7/8 in. candles. Ideal for use with our Victorian Lace Taper Candles shown on p. 96. (Plates and candles not included).
307-D-871

2. NEW FRESH FLOWER HOLDER
Insert between tiers to hold cascading blooms, greenery, pearl sprays, tulle puffs and more. Use with flower oasis (not included). 2 1/4 in. high, with 1 1/4 in. well.
205-D-8500 pk. of 2

3. NEW WIRE LACE SEPARATOR
Flowing filigree design gracefully separates wedding tiers. 2 in. high; 6 1/2 in. diameter.
303-D-870

4. NEW WIRE LACE UNITY CANDLEHOLDER
Openwork lace design holds candles up to 3 1/2 in. wide. 1 1/2 in. high.
120-D-870

5. NEW MINI LIGHTS
Softly illuminate floral arrangements, pillars and wedding ornaments. 10 bulbs on 20 in. long clear wire. Uses two AA batteries (not included)
1006-D-5

6. NEW WIRE LACE HEART PICK
Interwoven lilies and heart design enhances floral arrangements. 3 1/2 in. high with 3 1/2 in. pick stem.
1001-D-870

7. NEW WIRE LACE LOVEBIRDS PICK
Intricate flowing lines complement cake design. 3 1/2 in. high with 3 1/2 in. pick stem.
1001-D-872

8. NEW WIRE LACE BELL PICK
Free-hanging bell adds a distinctive touch. 4 in. high with 1 3/4 in. stem.
1001-D-871

NOTE: Some products offered in this publication may not be available in Canada.

ELEGANT ACCENTS

1. RUFFLE BOARDS®

Ready to use, It's a cake board and ruffle in one. The Ruffle Board® line features bleached white cake boards with all-white ruffling already attached.

8 in. (for 6 in. round cake)	415-D-950
10 in. (for 8 in. round cake)	415-D-960
12 in. (for 10 in. round cake)	415-D-970
14 in. (for 12 in. round cake)	415-D-980
16 in. (for 14 in. round cake)	415-D-990
18 in. (for 16 in. round cake)	415-D-1000

2. SHOW 'N SERVE CAKE BOARDS

Scalloped edge. Food-safe, grease-resistant coating.

8 in.	2104-D-1125	pk. of 10
10 in.	2104-D-1168	pk. of 10
12 in.	2104-D-1176	pk. of 8
14 in.	2104-D-1184	pk. of 6
14 x 20 in. Rectangle	2104-D-1230	pk. of 6

3. CAKE CIRCLES & BOARDS

Corrugated cardboard.

6 in. diameter	2104-D-64	pk. of 10
8 in. diameter	2104-D-80	pk. of 12
10 in. diameter	2104-D-102	pk. of 12
12 in. diameter	2104-D-129	pk. of 8
14 in. diameter	2104-D-145	pk. of 6
16 in. diameter	2104-D-160	pk. of 6
10 x 14 in.	2104-D-554	pk. of 6
13 x 19 in.	2104-D-552	pk. of 6

4. TUK-N-RUFFLE

Attach to serving tray or board with royal icing or tape. 60 ft. Bolt

Pink	802-D-702	per bolt
Blue	802-D-206	per bolt
White	802-D-1008	per bolt
6 ft. Package-White	802-D-1991	

DOILIES

Greaseproof quality makes a flawless presentation. Round and rectangular shapes have lace borders sized to fit around your decorated cakes.

5. GOLD DOILIES

4 in. Round	2104-D-90104	pk. of 24
8 in. Round	2104-D-90012	pk. of 12
10 in. Round	2104-D-90013	pk. of 6
12 in. Round	2104-D-90014	pk. of 4
10 x 14 in. Rec.	2104-D-90015	pk. of 4

6. SILVER DOILIES

4 in. Round	2104-D-90114	pk. of 24
8 in. Round	2104-D-90006	pk. of 12
10 in. Round	2104-D-90007	pk. of 6
12 in. Round	2104-D-90008	pk. of 4
10 x 14 in. Rec.	2104-D-90009	pk. of 4

7. WHITE DOILIES

4 in. Round	2104-D-89997	pk. of 40
5 in. Round	2104-D-89998	pk. of 36
6 in. Round	2104-D-89999	pk. of 28
8 in. Round	2104-D-90004	pk. of 16
10 in. Round	2104-D-90000	pk. of 12
12 in. Round	2104-D-90001	pk. of 8
14 in. Round	2104-D-90002	pk. of 8
10 x 14 in. Rec.	2104-D-90003	pk. of 8

8. FANCI-FOIL WRAP

Serving side has a non-toxic grease-resistant surface. FDA approved for use with food. Continuous roll: 20 in. x 15 ft.

Rose	804-D-124	White	804-D-191
Gold	804-D-183	Silver	804-D-167

PARCHMENT

Non-stick parchment lines pans, prevents sticking and withstands temperatures to 400°F.

9. RECTANGLES

Fits 9 x 13 in. pans (actual size $8^7/_8$ x $12^3/_4$ in.)
415-D-998 pk. of 15

Fits 11 x 15 in. pans (actual size $10^7/_8$ x $14^3/_4$ in.)
415-D-999 pk. of 15

10. PARCHMENT ROLL

Professional grade, silicone-treated parchment. Oven safe to 450°F, great in microwaves, too. Double roll contains 41 sq. feet. (15 in. x 33 ft.)
415-D-680 roll

11. SELECT-A-SIZE PARCHMENT CIRCLES

One sheet that helps you cut the exact size you need to line your pan – pre-marked circles can fit round pans from 6 to 12 in. Non-stick paper for easy release; oven-safe to 400°F.
415-D-994 pk. of 20

All white board . . . no brown edges!

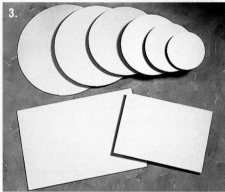

TUK-N-RUFFLE CONVERSION CHART

Find cake board size below; cut amount suggested.

Cake Board		Tuk-N-Ruffle	Cake Board		Tuk-N-Ruffle
Rounds	8 in.	2 ft. 6 in.	Squares	6 in.	2 ft. 4 in.
	10 in.	3 ft.		8 in.	3 ft.
	12 in.	3 ft. 7 in.		10 in.	3 ft. 8 in.
	14 in.	4 ft.		12 in.	4 ft. 4 in.
	16 in.	4 ft. 8 in.		14 in.	5 ft.
	18 in.	5 ft. 2 in.		16 in.	5 ft. 8 in.
Rectangles	7 x 11 in.	3 ft. 4 in.	Hexagons	6 in.	1 ft. 9 in.
	9 x 13 in.	4 ft.		9 in.	2 ft. 6 in.
	11 x 15 in.	4 ft. 8 in.		15 in.	4 ft. 6 in.
	12 x 18 in.	5 ft. 2 in.			
Ovals	$7^3/_4$ in.	1 ft. 9 in.	**Ovals**	$13^1/_2$ in.	3 ft. 3 in.
	$10^3/_4$ in.	2 ft. 6 in.		$16^1/_2$ in.	4 ft.

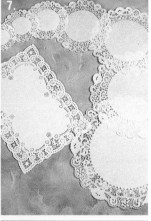

TOOLS & ACCESSORIES

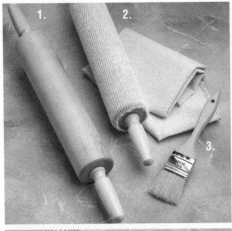

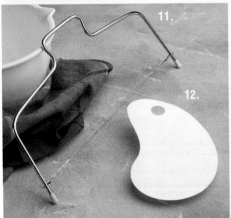

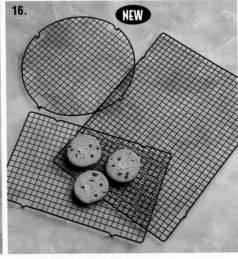

1. ROLLING PIN
Durable, non-absorbent rock maple with easy rolling nylon bearings. 10 x 2 1/2 in.
417-D-36

2. 2 PC. PASTRY CLOTH/ROLLING PIN COVER SET
Canvas cloths promote even rolling without sticking.
417-D-42

3. PASTRY BRUSH
Soft, natural bristles leave no marks when brushing liquids and glazes. 1 1/2 in.
417-D-54

4. 2 1/2 CUP LIQUID MEASURING CUP
Dishwasher and microwave safe, with easy-to-read measurements.
417-D-174

5-6. STAINLESS STEEL WHISKS
Long, solid handle provides control, 8 flexible wires make whipping easy.
5. 12 in.   417-D-78
6. 10 in.   417-D-72

7. 3 CUP STAINLESS STEEL SIFTER
Easy trigger-action and triple-mesh design provide fast, efficient sifting.
417-D-84

8. STAINLESS STEEL SUGAR/FLOUR SHAKER
Well-perforated cap evenly covers baked goods. Holds 6 oz. or 3/4 cup.
417-D-120

9. COOKIE SCOOP
Spring-action stainless steel scoop quickly forms and releases perfect portion of cookie dough. Scoop holds 1 oz.
417-D-150

10. 3 PC. MIXING BOWL SET
1 1/2 qt., 2 qt. and 3 qt. bowls with clearly marked measurements and easy-grip handles. Bottom rubber ring prevents slipping.
417-D-168 set

11. CAKE LEVELER
Levels, tortes cakes to 10 in. wide x 2 in. high.
415-D-815

12. SPATCH-IT SCRAPER
Gets to the bottom of the bowl. 6 1/2 x 4 in.
417-D-90

13. DECORATING TRIANGLE
Each side adds a different contoured effect to icing; easy to hold and use. 5 x 5 in. plastic.
417-D-162

14. DECORATING COMB
Easy-to-use tool forms ridges in icing for an elegantly finished cake. 12 x 1 1/2 in., plastic.
417-D-156

LARGE CAKES NEED OUR COOLING GRIDS!
Versatile grids handle tiers, character and sheet cakes up to 12 x 18 in. Tightly woven grids mean even the smallest cookies won't fall through; prevents cracking of crusts. Heavy-gauge chrome-plated steel protects counter-tops and tables from heat, while providing even support. Easy-cleaning non-stick also available.

15. CHROME-PLATED STEEL GRIDS
10 x 16 in.	2305-D-128
14 1/2 x 20 in.	2305-D-129
13 in. Round	2305-D-130
3 Pc. Stackable	2305-D-151

16. NON-STICK STEEL GRIDS
10 x 16 in.	2305-D-228
14 1/2 x 20 in.	2305-D-229
NEW 13 in. Round	2305-D-230

NOTE: Some products offered in this publication may not be available in Canada.

110

Wilton Tier Pan Sets keep your decorating options open! Use them together to create a high-rise masterpiece, or on their own for smaller celebrations. Durable anodized aluminum pans resist chips and flaking and are dishwasher safe.

1. 4 PC. (2 IN. DEEP) ROUND PAN SET
Set includes 6, 8, 10 and 12 in. aluminum pans.
2105-D-2101 set

2. 4 PC. (3 IN. DEEP) ROUND PAN SET
Set includes 8, 10, 12, 14 in. aluminum pans.
2105-D-2932 set

3. 4 PC. OVAL PAN SET
Set includes four 2 in. deep aluminum pans. Sizes are $7^3/_4$ x $5^5/_8$ in.; $10^3/_4$ x $7^7/_8$ in.; 13 x $9^7/_8$ in.; 16 x $12^3/_8$ in.
2105-D-2130 set

4. 4 PC. HEXAGON PAN SET
Set includes 6, 9, 12, 15 in. aluminum pans, 2 in. deep.
2105-D-3572 set

5. 4 PC. PETAL PAN SET
A pretty shape that's popular for showers, weddings and anniversaries. Set includes 6, 9, 12 and 15 in. 2 in. deep aluminum pans.
2105-D-2134 set

12 in. only 2105-D-5117

6. 4 PC. HEART PAN SET
Celebrate showers, weddings and more with the ultimate heart-shaped cake. Set includes 6, 9, 12 and $14^1/_2$ in. diameter aluminum pans. 2 in. deep.
2105-D-2131 set

INDIVIDUAL PANS AVAILABLE
6 in. 2105-D-4781
9 in. 2105-D-5176
12 in. 2105-D-5168

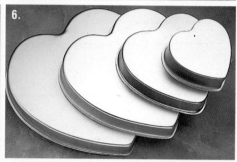

PROFESSIONAL-QUALITY desserts and cakes begin with the finest bakeware. Ovencraft™ Bakeware is the professional's choice – every pan is built to the highest standards for consistent, superior baking results.

— **EXTRA-THICK ALUMINUM** means Ovencraft™ pans provide the best heat distribution and will never warp. Compare these pans to ordinary bakeware and you'll see why Ovencraft™ pans can last for a lifetime.

— **DESIGNED FOR PRECISION:** each pan with special features which enhance its performance. Extra depth versus ordinary bakeware to reduce overflow...perfectly straight sides and 90° corners on squares and sheets for exact results...welded corners for strength.

— **A PROFESSIONAL FINISH.** Quality aluminum will not rust, discolor, chip or peel – it's the best finish for your baked goods. Cleans easily, releases food quickly and evenly.

OVENCRAFT™
Professional Bakeware

2 IN. DEEP ROUND PANS
Ideal for two-layer cakes and tier cakes.
6 in. 2105-D-5601
8 in. 2105-D-5602
9 in. 2105-D-5619
10 in. 2105-D-5603
12 in. 2105-D-5604
14 in. 2105-D-5605
16 in. 2105-D-5606

3 IN. DEEP ROUND PANS
Bake beautiful, tall cakes.
6 in. 2105-D-5620
8 in. 2105-D-5607
10 in. 2105-D-5608
12 in. 2105-D-5609
14 in. 2105-D-5610

3 IN. DEEP HALF-ROUND PAN
Use to bake an 18 in. round cake in conventional size oven.
18 in. 2105-D-5622

SQUARE PANS
Perfectly square corners and $2^3/_{16}$ inch depth produce professional quality cakes.
8 in. 2105-D-5611
10 in. 2105-D-5612
12 in. 2105-D-5613
14 in. 2105-D-5614

SHEET PANS
Endless options with this multi-use shape. Perfectly square corners. $2^3/_{16}$ in. deep.
9 x 13 in. 2105-D-5616
11 x 15 in. 2105-D-5617
12 x 18 in. 2105-D-5618

CREATING BEAUTIFUL TIER CAKES

Nothing impresses guests quite as much as a majestic tier cake. Perhaps because of its magnificence, a tier cake can be very intimidating to first time decorators. In reality, a tier cake is not as difficult to create as it looks.

TYPES AND METHODS OF TIER CAKE CONSTRUCTION

A tier cake is two, three, four or more single cakes put together. This "assembly" may be done in a number of ways. In this book, we include the most popular—from the quickest and easiest to the most elaborate. No one method creates a "prettier" cake than another. Every cake is beautiful and impressive in its own way. Just select the design you want and follow the easy step-by-step instructions for baking, decorating and assembling your cake. You will soon be delighted at what you have accomplished.

TO PREPARE TIERS FOR ASSEMBLY

• Bake, fill and ice tiers carefully before assembling. See p. 116 for baking and icing hints. Place base tier on a sturdy base plate or three or more thicknesses of corrugated cardboard. For heavy cakes, use 1/4 in. thick fiberboard or plywood. Base can be covered with Fanci-Foil Wrap and trimmed with Tuk-N-Ruffle or Doilies.
• Each tier in the cake must be on a cake circle or board cut to fit. Place a few strokes of icing on boards to secure cake.

THE FLOATING TIERS CAKE STAND METHOD OF ASSEMBLY

(Also use for Garden Cake Stand)

The quickest, easiest method of creating a tier cake is with the Wilton Floating Tiers Cake Stand. This stand is especially convenient for cheesecakes—and it can also be used for a variety of creative cake arrangements. The set includes stand, plus 8 in., 12 in. and 16 in. smooth-edged separator plates.

• To use, prepare tiers for assembly and set the decorated cakes on the separator plates. In general, the cakes should be 1 or 2 in. smaller than the plates. See specific designs in this book for other suggestions.
• The stand may be decorated with ribbons, bows, tulle and flowers. We suggest this be done before setting cakes on the stand.

CENTER COLUMN CONSTRUCTION WITH THE TALL TIER STAND

• Each cake involved in this type of construction should be placed on a cake circle or board (cut to fit) with a pre-cut center hole. To do this, trace pan shape on waxed paper. Note: To make positioning easier, place top tier on a board slightly larger than cake. Fold pattern into quarters to determine the exact center of each tier. Snip away the point to make a center hole (use cake corer as a guide to size). Trace hole pattern onto boards and cut out.
• Place all tiers on prepared cake boards, attaching with a few strokes of icing. Ice tiers smooth. Using hole pattern, mark centers on all cakes, except top tier. Core out cake centers by pushing the cake corer down to the cake base. Pull out and press cake out of corer.
• Screw a column to prepared base plate, attaching with the bottom column bolt from underneath the plate. Slip bottom tier over the column to rest on plate.
• The bottom of the plates will not sit level, so to decorate, set plates on the Flower Holder Ring, a pan or bowl. A damp, folded towel or piece of thin foam over the pan will prevent cake from slipping.
• Since the column cap nut attaches under the top tier, this cake must be positioned after assembling the Tall Tier Stand. Add base borders after assembling the top tier. Or you may place the top tier on a foil-covered cake circle so decorating can be done ahead.
• If using the 4-arm base stand, just attach either a 7 3/4 in. or 13 1/2 in. column to the center opening with the base nut included.
• To assemble at reception, position plate onto base column section and screw column tight. Continue adding tiers with columns. At top plate, secure columns with cap nut bolt. Position top tier and decorate base.

Hints: To keep balance, cut cakes on the Tall Tier Stand from top tier down.

Using a cake circle under your cake will prevent plates in set from getting scratched during cutting. Be sure to attach plates with dabs of icing to prevent slipping.

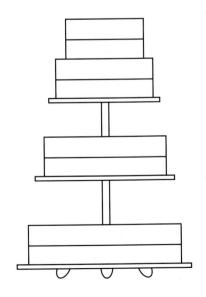

CONSTRUCTING TIER CAKES

To Dowel Rod Tiers for Stacked and Pillar Construction:

• Center a cake circle or plate one size smaller than the next tier on base tier and press it gently into icing to imprint and outline. Remove circle.

• Measure one dowel rod at the cake's lowest point within this circle. Using this dowel rod for measure, use pruning shears to cut dowel rods (to fit this tier) the same size. If the next tier is 10 in. or less, push seven ¼ in. dowel rods into the cake down to the base within the circle guide. Generally, the larger and more numerous the upper tiers, the more dowels needed. Very large cakes need ½ in. dowels in the base tier.

Dowel Rods

STACKED CONSTRUCTION

In this method, the tiers rise one above the other, with or without the use of pillars.

• When pillars are not used, each tier is placed directly on top of another. Dowel rod the bottom tier (See To Dowel Rod Cake For Stacked and Pillar Construction above). Center a cake circle one size smaller than the tier to be added, on top

Stacked

of the base tier (example: 9 in. circle under a 10 in. tier). Position the tier. Repeat the procedure for each additional tier. To decorate, start at the top tier and work down.

• To keep stacked tiers stable, sharpen one end of a dowel rod and push it through all the tiers and cardboard circles to base of the bottom tier.

Pillar

PILLAR CONSTRUCTION

With this construction, the tiers are separated by pillars. Dowel rods are inserted into the lower tiers to bear the weight of the tiers above. Pillar construction may be used to lift all the tiers or it may be combined with stacked construction to create very beautiful cakes.

• Dowel rod tiers. (See instructions above.) Optional: Press pegs into separator plates to prevent slipping (never substitute pegs for dowel rods).

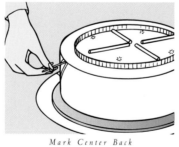

Mark Center Back

Position separator plates on supporting tiers, making sure that pillar projections on each tier will line up with pillars below. Mark centerbacks of tiers. Decorate tiers.

• At reception, align pillar projections and assemble tiers on pillars.

FAST AND EASY PUSH-IN LEG/ SPIKED PILLAR CONSTRUCTION

This is very similar to pillar construction, except that the legs inserted into the separator plates are pushed right through the tiers down to the plate below. Dowel rods are not needed. This method can also be used with stacked construction.

Mark Where Legs Go

• Ice cakes on cake circles.

• Mark where the legs will go by centering the separator for the tier above (projections down) and gently pressing onto the tier below. Lift the plate off.

• Repeat this procedure for each tier (except the top).

• Position upper tiers on separator plates. Decorate tiers.

• To assemble: Insert legs at marks into cake. Place plate and cake on legs. Push straight down until legs touch cake board. Continue adding tiers in this way until cake is assembled.

Push-in leg

• When stacking tiers, be sure to double the cake circles between tiers to prevent the pillars from going through.

CREATIVE COMBINATIONS AND DESIGNS

Many beautiful tier cakes can be created by combining pillar and stacked tier construction. With this combination, two or more tiers are stacked and and one or more is lifted by pillars. Usually, two tiers are stacked for the base, and the top tier is raised with pillars, but any combination may be used. Several exciting tier cakes constructed in the combination method are included in this book.

ASSEMBLING TIER CAKES WITH STAIRWAYS

*Filigree stairways are a beautiful way to pull your multi-tiered masterpiece together.
Even a two-tiered cake can look elegant and substantial when ornamented with stairways and bridges.
They become an integral part of your design, whether decorated with icing flowers or used
to provide a graceful platform for bridesmaid and groomsman figurines and your wedding ornament.*

HOW TO ATTACH THE STAIRWAY

Putting stairs together is easy! It's best to have a partner hold the stairway as you shift position of the cakes. Your partner can also help you check that stairs stand at the proper height in relation to your cakes. You need only remember two measurements when assembling your stairways:

I. For stairways which will not be joined to a bridge, allow for an 8 in. difference in height from top to bottom of stairway.

2. For stairways which will be joined to a bridge, allow for a 7 in. difference in height from top to bottom of stairway.

STAIRWAYS WITH BRIDGES

Simply slide the tops of the stairways into slots below the surface of the bridge. Set main cake and any satellite cakes in approximate position. Ask your partner to hold the assembled stairway and bridge above the cakes. Shift the satellites as necessary. Gently press the bridge until its base touches the top tier of the main cake. Allow the bottom of the stairway to rest on the satellite cake.

STAIRWAYS ONLY

Arrange main cake and any satellite cakes in approximate positions. Have partner hold stairway above cakes and shift the cakes as necessary. Gently insert top of stairway into top side of main cake until stairway is touching side of cake. Allow bottom of stairway to rest on satellite cake.

CAKES WITH STAIRWAYS NOT ATTACHED TO BRIDGE

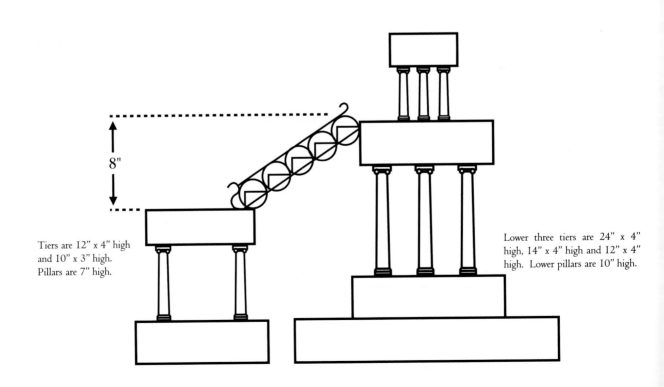

8"

Tiers are 12" x 4" high and 10" x 3" high. Pillars are 7" high.

Lower three tiers are 24" x 4" high, 14" x 4" high and 12" x 4" high. Lower pillars are 10" high.

CAKES WITH STAIRWAYS ATTACHED TO BRIDGE

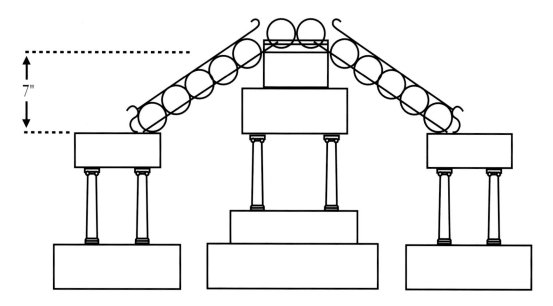

7"

Tiers are 12" x 4" high
and 8" x 3" high.
Pillars are 7" high.

Tiers are 16" x 4" high, 12" x 3"
high, and 10" x 4" high, and
6" x 3" high. Pillars are 7" high.

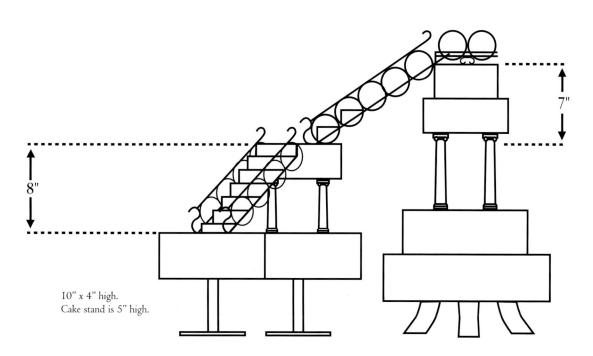

8"

7"

10" x 4" high.
Cake stand is 5" high.

Tiers are 12" x 4" high
and 8" x 3" high.
Pillars are 5" high.
Cake stand is 5" high.

Tiers are 16" x 4" high, 12" x 4"
high, 8" x 3" high and 6" x 3" high,
and 6" x 8" high. Pillars are 7" high,
legs under base plate 3" high.

BAKING

GREASE	FLOUR	SHAKE	PLACE RACK	REMOVE

• Preheat oven to temperature specified in recipe or on packaged mix.

• Thoroughly grease the inside of each pan with solid vegetable shortening or use a vegetable cooking spray. Use a pastry brush to spread the shortening evenly. Be sure sides, corners and all indentations are completely covered.

• Sprinkle flour inside of pan and shake back and forth so the flour covers all the greased surfaces. Tap out excess flour and if any shiny spots remain, touch up with more shortening and flour. This step is essential in preventing your cake from sticking. If you prefer, the bottom may be lined with waxed paper after greasing. This eliminates flouring the pan. Your cake will unmold easily, but with more crumbs.

• Bake the cake according to temperature specifications in recipe or on package instructions. Remove cake from oven and let cool 10 minutes in pan on a cake rack. Larger cakes over 12 in. diameter may need to cool 15 minutes.

• So cake sits level and to prevent cracking, while in pan or after unmolding, cut away the raised center portion with a serrated knife. Hint: Our Bake-Even Strips help prevent crowns from forming. To unmold cake, place cake rack against cake and turn both rack and pan over. Remove pan carefully. If pan will not release, return it to a warm oven (250°F) for a few minutes, then repeat procedure. Cool cake completely, at least 1 hour. Brush off loose crumbs and frost.

BAKING HINTS

• If you like to bake ahead, do so. Your baked cake can be frozen up to three months wrapped in heavy-duty foil.

• Always thaw cake completely before icing. Keep it wrapped to prevent it from drying out. Your cake will still be fresh and easy to ice because it will be firm. It will also have fewer crumbs.

• Packaged, two-layer cake mixes usually yield 4 to 6 cups of batter, but formulas change, so always measure. Here's a handy guide: One 2-layer cake mix will make: two 8 in. round layers, one 10 in. round layer.

• If you're in doubt as to how many cups of batter you need to fill a pan, measure the cups of water it will hold first and use this number as a guide. Then, if you want a cake with high sides, fill the pan ⅔ full of batter. For slightly thinner cake layers, fill ½ full.

• For 3-in. deep pans, we recommend pound, fruit or pudding-added cake batters. Fill pan half full only.

TAILOR CAKES TO THE SIZE YOU WANT

Don't be put off if the design you like serves too many or too few. It's easy to stretch or shrink most cakes to accommodate your party.

INCREASE OR DECREASE TIER SIZES: Any cake whose smallest tier measures 8" or more in diameter may be modified to serve fewer by decreasing each tier diameter by 2". Or, to serve more, increase each tier diameter by 2".

See serving chart (p. 121) to estimate your new serving amount. Remember, your plate size must change along with your cake size.

ADD SATELLITE CAKES: Expand your tiered cake, by surrounding it with individual cakes which echo its design. See pgs. 34 and 78 for satellite designs which may work for you.

SERVE SHEET CAKES: Rather than alter the size of your cake, hold additional sheet cakes in the kitchen (your guests will never know).

ADD "DUMMY" TIERS: If the design you want is too big for your wedding, create base tiers in styrofoam. Cover these first in royal icing, let dry, then ice in buttercream. Styrofoam is available, and can be cut to the size you need, in most craft stores. You may also use cardboard cake circles, taped together to form the proper height, wrapped in foil and iced in royal, then buttercream.

FILLING & ICING

By following our five-easy-steps icing method, you'll get the results you want.

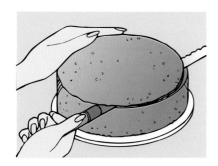

1. LEVELING
There are two ways to remove the slight crown your baked cake will have. Cool cake for 10 minutes in the pan. Using a serrated knife, with a sawing motion, carefully slice off the raised center. Or, unmold the cake and allow to cool completely on rack. Invert so that its brown top crust is uppermost and trim away the crust for a flat surface. Our Bake-Even Strips will help prevent crowns from forming on basic shaped wedding cakes.

2. FILLING LAYERS
Place one cake layer on a cake board or circle atop a cake stand or plate, top side up. Hint: to prevent cake from shifting, smear a few strokes of icing on base surface before positioning cake. Fit bag with coupler and fill with icing. Make a dam by squeezing out a band of icing or filling about ¾ in. high around the top. (If coupler has a slot opening on the side, keep this slot facing downward as you squeeze.) With your spatula, spread icing, jam, pudding or other filling in center. Position top layer with bottom side up.

3. ICING THE TOP
Thin your buttercream icing with light corn syrup (approximately 2 teaspoons for each cup). The consistency is correct when your spatula glides over the icing. With large spatula, place mound of icing in center of top and spread across cake, pushing excess down onto sides. Always keep spatula on the icing surface. Touching the cake will mix in crumbs. Hint: To keep your serving base free of icing, place 3 in. wide strips of waxed paper under each side of cake.

4. ICING THE SIDES
Cover the sides with excess icing from the top, adding more icing if necessary. Work from the top down, forcing any loose crumbs to the cake base. Again, be sure spatula touches only icing. You'll find that an angled spatula is ideal for icing sides.

Use the same procedures shown here for sheet cakes, heart, oval, square and other shaped cakes with flat surfaces.

5. SMOOTH SIDES & TOP
Smooth the side of the cake first, using the edge of a large spatula. Hold the spatula upright against the side of the cake, and slowly spin the stand without lifting the spatula from the cake's surface. Return excess frosting to the bowl.
Smooth the top of the cake last, again using the edge of the large spatula. Sweep the edge of the spatula from the rim of the cake to its center; then lift it off and remove the excess icing.

HOW TO TINT ICING
Start with white icing and add the color a little at a time until you achieve the shade you desire. Use a toothpick to add icing color; (use more depending on amount of icing). Hint: Tint a small amount of icing first, then mix in with remainder of white icing. Colors intensify or darken in buttercream icings 1 to 2 hours after mixing, so keep this in mind when you're tinting icing. You can always add extra color to deepen the icing color, but it's difficult to lighten once it's tinted. Use White-White Icing Color to make your buttercream icing made with butter or margarine the purest snow-white!

Always mix enough of any one color icing. If you're going to decorate a cake with pink flowers and borders, color enough icing for both. It's difficult to duplicate an exact shade of any color.

ICING RECIPES

BUTTERCREAM ICING

½ cup solid vegetable shortening
½ cup butter or margarine*
1 teaspoon Clear Vanilla Extract
4 cups sifted confectioners sugar
  (approx. 1 lb.)
2 tablespoons milk**

Cream butter and shortening with electric mixer. Add vanilla. Gradually add sugar, one cup at a time, beating well on medium speed. Scrape sides and bottom of bowl often. When all sugar has been mixed in, icing will appear dry. Add milk and beat at medium speed until light and fluffy. Keep icing covered with a damp cloth until ready to use. Refrigerated in an airtight container, this icing can be stored 2 weeks. Rewhip before using.
MAKES: 3 cups.

*Substitute all-vegetable shortening and ½ teaspoon Wilton Butter Extract for pure white icing and stiffer consistency.

**Add 3-4 tablespoons light corn syrup per recipe to thin for icing cake.

CHOCOLATE BUTTERCREAM

Add ¾ cup cocoa or three 1 oz. unsweetened chocolate squares, melted, and an additional 1 to 2 tablespoons milk to recipe. Mix until well blended.

ROYAL EGG WHITE ICING RECIPE*

3 egg whites (room temperature)
4 cups confectioners sugar
  (approx. 1 lb.)
½ teaspoon cream of tartar

Beat all ingredients at high speed for 7 to 10 mintues. Use immediately. Rebeating will not restore texture.
MAKES: 2½ cups.

SNOW-WHITE BUTTERCREAM

⅔ cup water
4 tablespoons Wilton Meringue
  Powder Mix
12 cups sifted confectioners sugar
  (approximately 3 lbs.)
1¼ cups solid shortening
¾ teaspoon salt
½ teaspoon Almond Extract
½ teaspoon Clear Vanilla Extract
¼ teaspoon Butter Flavor

Combine water and meringue powder; whip at high speed until peaks form. Add 4 cups sugar, one cup at a time, beating after each addition at low speed. Alternately add shortening and remainder of sugar. Add salt and flavorings; beat at low speed until smooth.
MAKES: 7 cups.

Note: Recipe may be doubled or cut in half. If cut in half, yield is 2⅔ cups.

STABILIZED WHIPPED CREAM ICING

1 teaspoon unflavored gelatin
4 teaspoons cold water
1 cup heavy whipping cream
¼ cup confectioners sugar
½ teaspoon Clear Vanilla Extract

Combine gelatin and cold water in small saucepan. Let stand until thick. Place over low heat, stirring constantly, just until gelatin dissovles. Remove from heat and cool (gelatin should be cool but still liquid). Whip cream, sugar, and vanilla until slightly thickened. While beating slowly, gradually add gelatin to whipped cream mixture. Whip at high speed until stiff.
MAKES: 2 cups.

Cakes iced with whipped cream must be stored in the refrigerator. Hint: Cream may be whipped in a food processor with metal blade. It will have less volume and be velvety smooth.

ROYAL ICING

3 level tablespoons Meringue Powder
4 cups sifted confectioners sugar
  (approx. 1 lb.)
6 tablespoons water*

Beat all ingredients at low speed for 7 to 10 minutes (10 to 12 minutes at high speed for portable mixer) until icing forms peaks.
MAKES: 3 cups.

*When using larger countertop mixer or for stiffer icing, use 1 tablespoon less water.

ROLL-OUT COOKIE DOUGH

1 cup butter
1 cup sugar
1 large egg
2 tsps. baking powder
1 tsp. vanilla
3 cups flour

Preheat oven to 400° F. In a large bowl, cream butter and sugar with an electric mixer. Beat in egg and vanilla. Add baking powder and flour, one cup at a time, mixing after each addition. The dough will be very stiff; blend last flour in by hand (if dough becomes too stiff, add water a teaspoon at a time). Do not chill dough. Divide dough into 2 balls. On a floured surface, roll each ball into a circle approximately 12 inches in diameter and ⅛ in thick. Dip cutters in flour before each use. Bake cookies on an ungreased cookie sheet on top rack of oven for 6-7 minutes, or until cookies are lightly browned.

ROLLED FONDANT RECIPE

I tablespoon unflavored gelatin
¼ cup cold water
½ cup Wilton Glucose
I tablespoon Wilton Glycerin
2 tablespoons solid vegetable
   shortening
2 lbs. confectioners sugar
2-3 drops liquid food color and
   flavoring, as desired

Combine gelatin and cold water; let stand until thick. Place gelatin mixture in top of double boiler and heat until dissolved. Add glucose and glycerin, mix well. Stir in shortening and just before completely melted, remove from heat, add flavoring and color. Mixture should cool until lukewarm. Next, place I lb. confectioners sugar in a bowl and make a well. Pour the lukewarm gelatin mixture into the well and stir with a wooden spoon, mixing in sugar and adding more, a little at a time, until stickiness disappears. Knead in remaining sugar. Knead until the fondant is smooth, pliable and does not stick to your hands. If fondant is too soft, add more sugar; it too stiff, add water (a drop at a time). Use fondant immediately or store in air tight container in refrigerator. When ready to use, bring to room temperature and knead again until soft. This recipe yields enough to cover a 10 x 4-in. high cake. If you want to save time, and achieve a beautiful fondant cake, use Wilton Ready-To-Use Rolled Fondant.

TO ROLL FONDANT

Spray work surface and rolling pin with vegetable oil pan spray and dust with a mixture of confectioners sugar and cornstarch. Here are two ways to prepare cake for fondant. Coat with piping gel or apricot glaze, then cover with rolled marzipan. Coat again with piping gel or glaze. Add fondant. Or ice cake with buttercream icing, let set, then cover with rolled fondant or use new Wilton Ready-To-Use Rolled Fondant. Roll out fondant into a circle the diameter of the cake plus double the height of the cake you are covering. As you roll, lift and move the fondant to prevent it from sticking to the surface.

Gently lift fondant over rolling pin and place over cake. Smooth and shape fondant on cake, using palm of hand.

If large air bubbles are trapped under fondant, prick with a pin and continue to smooth. Trim excess from base. A fondant-covered cake may be kept for several days.

COLOR FLOW ICING RECIPE

(Full-strength for Outlining)
¼ cup water + I teaspoon
I lb. sifted confectioners sugar (4 cups)
2 tablespoons Wilton Color Flow
   Icing Mix

In an electric mixer, using grease-free utensils, blend all ingredients on low speed for 5 minutes. If using hand mixer, use high speed. Color Flow icing "crusts" quickly, so keep it covered with a damp cloth while using. Stir in desired icing color. In order to fill an outlined area, this recipe must be thinned with ½ teaspoon of water per ¼ cup of icing (just a few drops at a time as you near proper consistency). Color Flow is ready for filling in outlines when a smalamount dropped into the mixture takesa full count of ten to disappear. Use grease-free spoon or spatula to stir slowly.

Note: Color Flow designs take a long time to dry, so plan to do your Color Flow piece at least 2-3 days in advance.

COLOR FLOW ICING

• Tape pattern and waxed paper overlay to your work surface. (The back of a cookie pan makes a great work surface.) Use full-strength Color Flow icing and tip 2 or 3 to outline the pattern with desired colors. If you're going to use the same color icing to fill in the outlines, let the icing outlines dry a few minutes until they "crust." If you're going to fill in icing that differs in color from the outlines, then let outlines dry thoroughly (I-2 hours) before filling in.

• Thin icing for filling in pattern outlines as specified in recipe. Don't use a tip for filling in outlines; instead, cut a very small opening in end of parchment bag. Begin filling in along the edges of the outline first, squeezing gently and letting the icing flow up to the outline almost by itself. Work quickly; filling in design from the outside edges in and from top to bottom. If you have several outlined sections, fill in one at a time. If you're filling in a large area, have two half-full parchment bags ready, otherwise icing could "crust" before you finish filling in the pattern.

Hint: Since buttercream icing will break down color flow, either position color flow decoration on cake shortly before serving or place a piece of plastic wrap, cut to fit, on area first and set atop sugar cubes.

WEDDING CAKE CUTTING GUIDE

This chart shows how to cut popular shaped wedding tiers into pieces approximately 1 in. x 2 in. by two layers high (about 4 in.). Even if you prefer a larger serving size, the order of cutting is still the same.

The first step in cutting is to remove the top tier, and then begin the cutting with the 2nd tier followed by the 3rd, 4th and so on. The top tier is usually saved for the first anniversary, so it is not figured into the serving amount.

To cut round tiers, move in two inches from the tier's outer edge; cut a circle and then slice 1 in. pieces within the circle. Now move in another 2 in., cut another circle, slice 1 in. pieces and so on until the tier is completely cut. The center core of each tier and the small top tier can be cut into halves, 4ths, 6ths and 8ths, depending on size.

Cut petal-shaped tiers similar to round tiers as diagram shows.

Cut hexagon tiers similar to round tiers.

To cut heart-shaped tiers, divide the tiers vertically into halves, quarters, sixths or eighths. Within rows, slice one inch pieces of cake.

To cut square tiers, move in 2 in. from the outer edge and cut across. Then slice 1 in. pieces of cake. Now move in another 2 in. and slice again until the entire tier is cut.

To cut oval tiers, move in 2 in. from the outer edge and cut across. Then slice 1 in. pieces of cake. Now move in another 2 in. and slice again until the entire tier is cut.

Cutting guides for shapes not shown can be found in other Wilton publications.

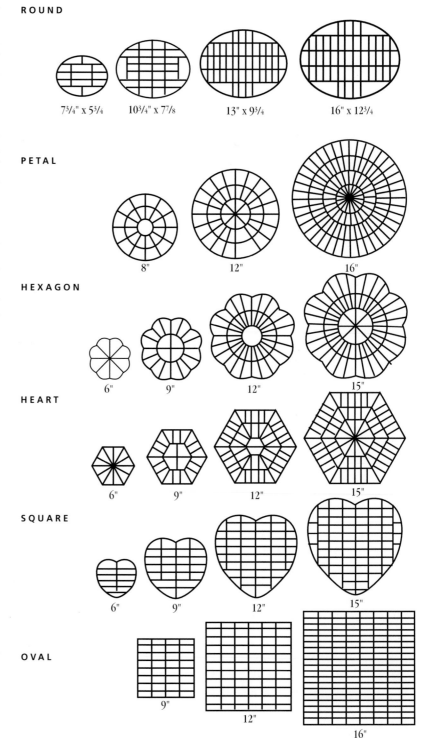

ROUND

$7\frac{3}{4}$" x $5\frac{3}{4}$ $10\frac{3}{4}$" x $7\frac{7}{8}$ 13" x $9\frac{3}{4}$ 16" x $12\frac{3}{4}$

PETAL

8"   12"   16"

HEXAGON

6"   9"   12"   15"

HEART

6"   9"   12"   15"

SQUARE

6"   9"   12"   15"

OVAL

9"   12"   16"

WEDDING CAKE DATA

One cake mix yields 4 to 6 cups of batter. Pans are usually filled ½ to ⅔ full; 3 in. deep pans should be filled only ½ full. Batter amounts on this chart are for pans two-thirds full of batter. Icing amounts are very general and will vary with consistency, thickness applied and tips used. These amounts allow for top and base borders and a side ruffled border. For large cakes, always check for doneness after they have baked for one hour.

Number of servings are intended as a guide only.

HINTS FOR ASSEMBLING & TRANSPORTING TIERED CAKES

• Before placing separator plate or cake circle atop another tier, sprinkle a little confectioners sugar or coconut flakes to prevent plate or circle from sticking. Letting icing crust a bit before positioning plate on cake will also prevent sticking.
• You will have less crumbs when icing if cakes are baked a day in advance.
• When filling or torting large layers, use less than you usually would. Your dam of icing should also be far enough from edge so filling doesn't form a bubble.
• The cake icer tip (789) is an invaluable timesaver in icing wedding tiers.
• The 16 in. bevel pan takes 1½ cake mixes. So your beveled sides bake properly, pull batter out from center to add depth to the sides.
• When transporting tiers, place cakes on damp towels or carpet foam and drive carefully. Never transport fully assembled cake.
• Some of the plates of the Tall Tier Stand will not sit level when not on the stand. Pack atop crumpled foil, tissue or towels when transporting. To decorate, set plates on pan or bowl. The column cap nut of the Tall Tier Stand attaches under the top tier cake. Therefore, this cake must be positioned after assembling

Pan Shape	Size	# Servings 2 Layer	Cups Batter/ I Layer 2"	Baking Temps.	Baking Time Minutes	Approx. Cups Icing to Frost and Decorate
Oval	7¾ x 5¾"	13	2½	350°	25-30	3
	10¾ x 7⅞"	30	5½	350°	25-30	4
	13 x 9¾"	44	8	350°	25-30	5½
	16 x 12¾"	70	11	325°	25-30	7½
Round	6"	14	2	350°	25-30	3
	8"	25	3	350°	30-35	4
	9"	32	5⅓	350°	30-35	4½
	10"	39	11	350°	35-40	5
	12"	56	7½	350°	35-40	6
	14"	77	10	325°	50-55	7¼
	16"	100	15	325°	55-60	8¾
Round 3" Deep (# Servings for 1 layer)	8"	15	5	325°	60-65	7¼
	10"	24	8	325°	75-80	4¾
	12"	33	11	325°	75-80	5¾
	14"	45	15	325°	75-80	7
Half Round 2" layer 3" layer	18"	127† 92††	9* 12*	325° 325°	60-65 60-65	10½ 10½
Petal	6"	8	1½	350°	25-30	3½
	9"	20	3½	350°	35-40	6
	12"	38	7	350°	35-40	7¾
	15"	62	12	325°	50-55	11
Hexagon	6"	12	1¾	350°	30-35	2¾
	9"	22	3½	350°	35-40	4¾
	12"	50	6	350°	40-45	5¾
	15"	72	11	325°	40-45	8¾
Heart	6"	11	1½	350°	25	2½
	9"	24	3½	350°	30	4½
	12"	48	8	350°	30	5¾
	15"	76	11½	325°	40	8¾
Square	6"	18	2	350°	25-30	3½
	8"	32	4	350°	35-40	4½
	10"	50	6	350°	35-40	6
	12"	72	10	350°	40-45	7½
	14"	98	13½	350°	45-50	9½
	16"	128	15½	350°	45-50	11
	18"	162	18	350°	50-55	13

*Batter for each half round pan.   †Four half rounds.   ††Two half rounds.

the Tall Tier Stand. Place top tier on a cake circle slightly larger then the cake to make positioning easier. Add base borders after assembling the top tier.
• To keep balance, cut cakes on the Tall Tier Stand from top tier down.
• To divide tiers, use the Cake Dividing Set. The Wheel Chart makes it easy to mark 2 in. intervals on 6 to 18 in. diameter cakes. The triangle marker gives precise spacing for stringwork and garlands. The raised lines on separator plates can also be followed for each dividing.
• When using Spiked Pillars and stacked construction, double cake boards or use separator plates between layers to prevent the weight of tiers from causing the pillars to pierce through cake.

CHURCH PATTERNS FOR
AUTUMN'S ILLUSION, PGS. 60-61

STEEPLE

CHURCH FRONT & BACK

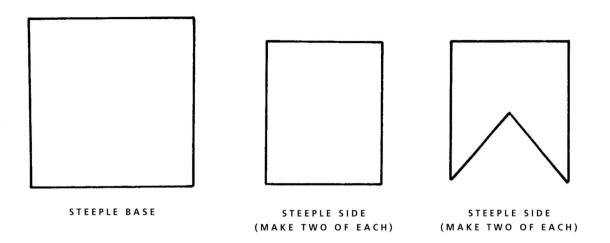

STEEPLE BASE

STEEPLE SIDE
(MAKE TWO OF EACH)

STEEPLE SIDE
(MAKE TWO OF EACH)

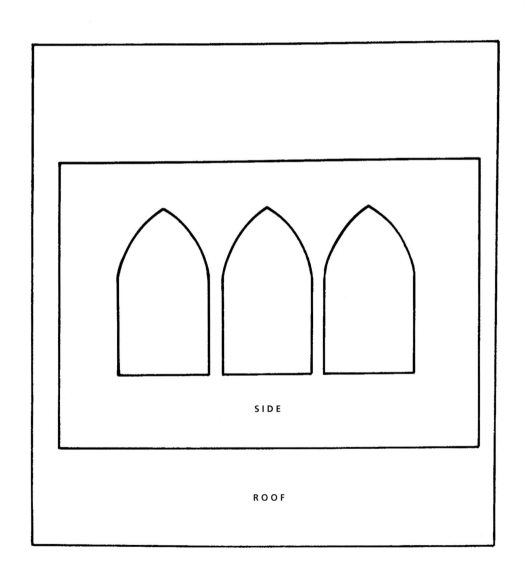

SIDE

ROOF

LETTERS PATTERN FOR DANCING ON AIR, PGS. 52-53
FOR SMALL LETTERS, ENLARGE PATTERN 170%. FOR LARGE LETTERS, ENLARGE PATTERN 240%

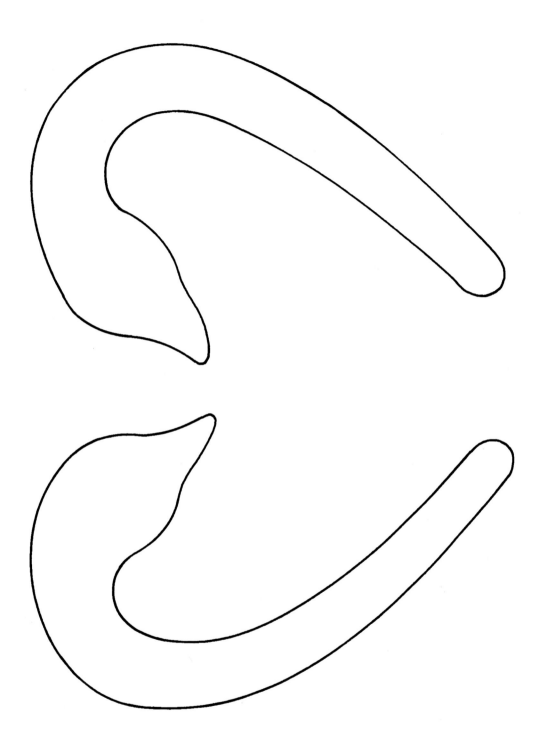

SWAN PATTERN FOR LOVE BIRDS, PGS. 54-55

HEXAGONS, DOOR AND WINDOWS
FOR DREAM CASTLE, PGS. 72-75

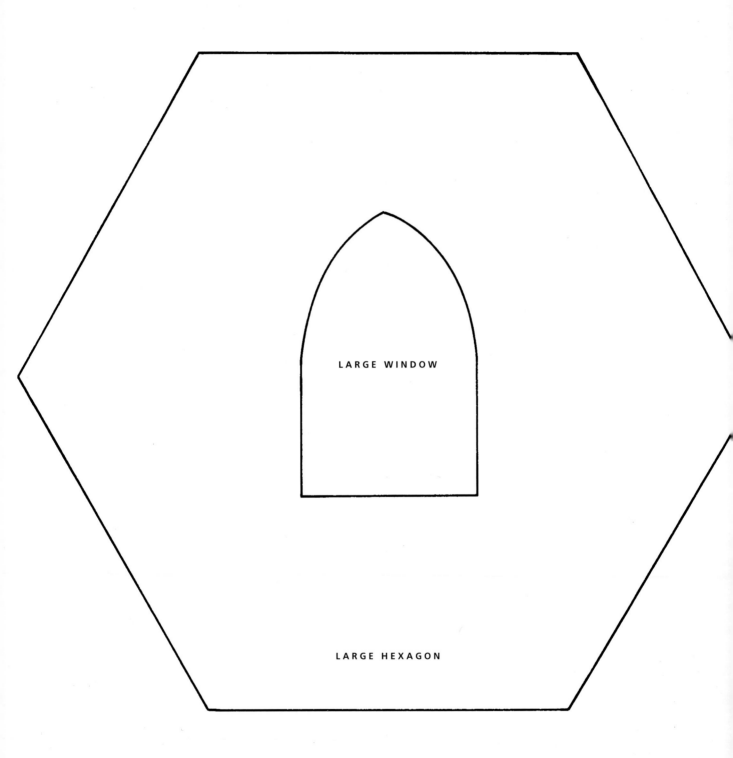

LARGE WINDOW

LARGE HEXAGON

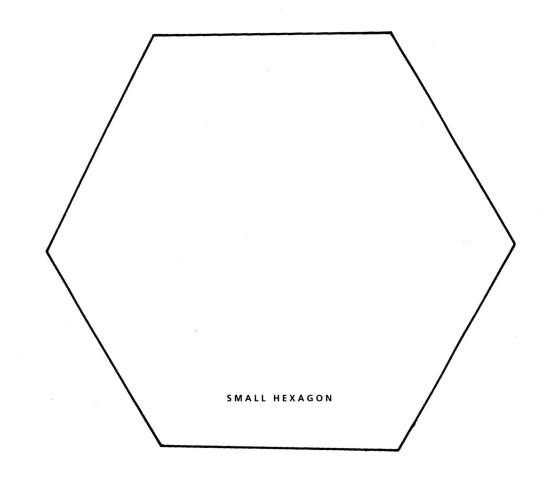

SMALL HEXAGON

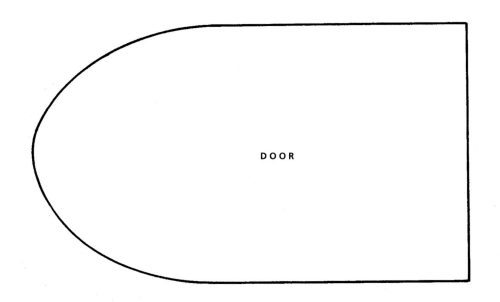

DOOR

SMALL
WINDOW

SCALLOP PATTERNS
FOR SWEET REVERIE, PGS. 4-5

A

SCALLOP PATTERN
TOP TIER - 1 OF 2

A

SCALLOP PATTERN
TOP TIER - 2 OF 2

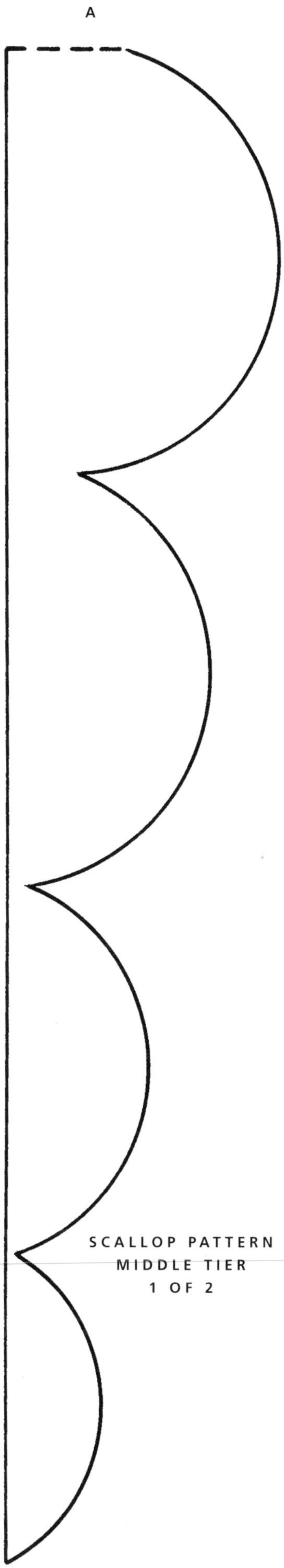

A

SCALLOP PATTERN
MIDDLE TIER
1 OF 2

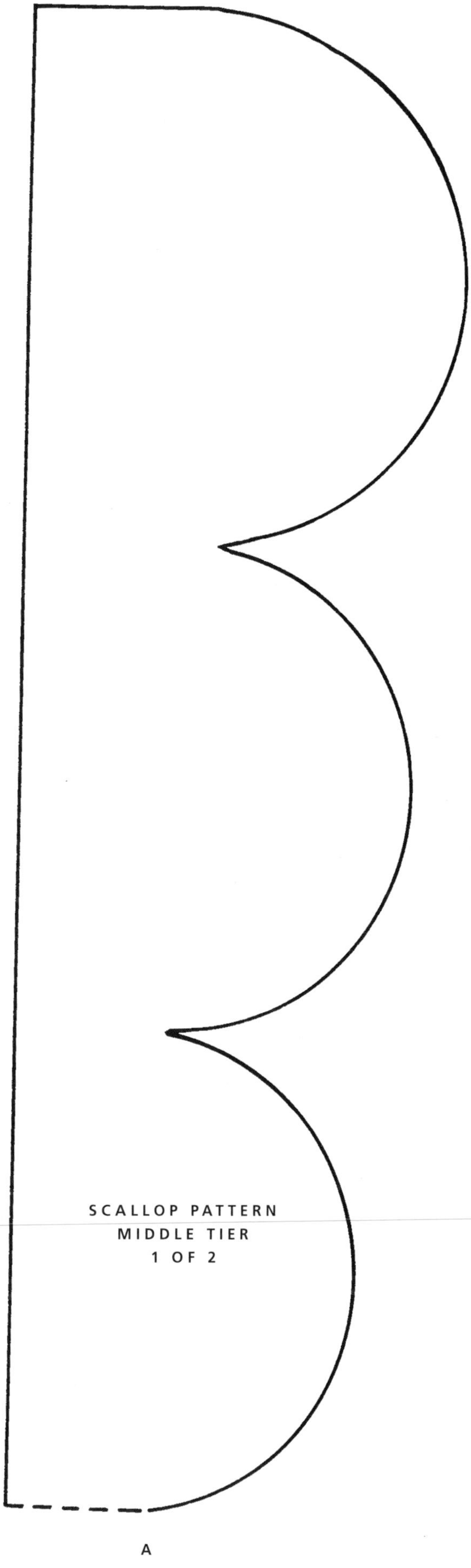

SCALLOP PATTERN
MIDDLE TIER
1 OF 2

A

BOTTOM TIER
1 OF 3

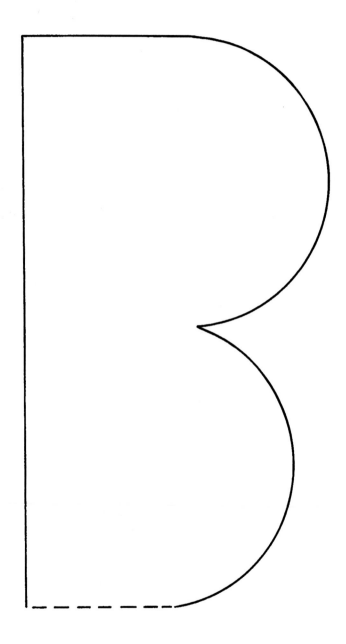

A

C

BOTTOM TIER
2 OF 3

BOTTOM TIER
3 OF 3

B

LOVE PLAQUE, SINGLE ROSE, ROSE CLUSTER PATTERNS FOR A LOVE FOR THE AGES, PGS. 12-13

SMALL, MEDIUM, LARGE
FILIGREE PATTERNS
FOR FILIGREE FANTASY, PGS. 8-9

CREDITS

Creative Director	Richard Tracy
Creative Consultant	Emy Schwartz
Cake Design	Steve Rocco
Cake Decorating	Susan Matusiak
	Mary Gavenda
	Corky Kagay
	Nancy Suffolk Guerine
	Judy Wysocki
	Darcy Simenson
Editor	Jeff Shankman
Writer	Anne Cummings Lawson
Design & Production	Bullet Communications, Inc.
Production Coordination	Laura Fortin
	Mary Stahulak
Photography	Jeff Carter
Photo Stylist	Jenny Nagle

THE GARDEN WEDDING

*Photographed at the home
of Mary and John Stachnik*

Recipes & Food Stylist	Zella Junkin
Florals	Kehoe Designs
Linens	Linen Effects
Rentals	Hall's Rental Service, Inc.

THE AT-HOME RECEPTION

*Photographed at the home
of Donna Almerico*

Recipes & Food Stylist	Zella Junkin
Florals	Kehoe Designs
Rentals	Hall's Rental Service, Inc.

THE HOTEL RECEPTION

*Photographed at The Four Seasons,
Chicago, Illinois*

Menu Created and Executed By	Mark Baker, Executive Chef, Four Seasons Hotel
Executive Sous Chef	Douglas Anderson
Banquet Sous Chef	James McNally
Florals	Ronsley
Linens	BBJ Boutique Linens
Rentals	Hall's Rental Service, Inc.

Our product selection is updated regularly. Some products shown in this book may no longer be available. To see the latest selection of Wilton wedding products, see your Wilton dealer or the most recent edition of the Wilton Yearbook Of Cake Decorating. Or visit our website: www.wedding.wilton.com

You may also write or call:
Wilton Industries
Caller Service #1604
2240 W. 75th St. Woodridge, IL 60517
800-794-5866
Fax: 888-824-9520
E-mail: info@wilton.com

For photography purposes, most designs were decorated with royal icing. Printed in U.S.A.